Praise for This Book

"This is really two great books in one. An eminently sensible guide packed with wisdom and practical tips grounded in professional experience and up-to-date scientific research. And a workbook with easy, yet valuable, exercises to help parents implement fifteen steps to ensure their children's well-being. Handy 'snap' reads conveniently highlight the main takeaways. These prescriptions alone are worth the price of admission."

> — Dr. Richard A. Warshak
> Past clinical professor of psychiatry, University of Texas Southwestern
> Medical Center
> Author, *Divorce Poison: How to Protect Your Family from Bad-mouthing and Brainwashing*
> Richardson, Texas

"This book is a must-read for any parent navigating unchartered waters and wanting to find a healthy passageway for their children. With clarity and concision, Part I provides vital information arising out of decades of research on risk and resiliency factors, which every parent needs to know to be able to foster healthy child adjustment. Using concrete goals combined with practical worksheets, Part II identifies fifteen positive steps including what to do and what to avoid so that parents can protect their children from adult conflict, foster healthy child adjustment, and support positive relationships with both parents. This quick-and-easy read is sure to prove invaluable to parents and their children and a great resource for parent education courses. Don't miss out on the twenty mini videos, a bonus, available at the Kids First website!"

> — Barbara Jo Fidler, PhD
> Registered psychologist, mediator, parenting coordinator
> Co-author, *Children Who Resist Postseparation Parental Contact: A Differential Approach for Legal and Mental Health Professionals*
> Toronto, Canada

"This book brilliantly distills the best relevant social science and applies it to the practical challenges that families face as they re-structure after a parental breakup. The wisdom provided for parents is delivered in a well-organized, reader-friendly format that is engaging and hands-on, utilizing worksheets and examples of approaches to a myriad of all-too-common coparenting scenarios. Dr. Muklewicz delivers on the hopeful premise that parents who are armed with evidence-based and solution-oriented advice can avoid harm to their children and successfully navigate this family transition."

> — Matthew J. Sullivan, PhD
> Co-founder, Overcoming Barriers, Inc.
> 2019-2020 president, Association of Family and Conciliation Courts (AFCC)
> Author, *Overcoming the Alienation Crisis: 33 Coparenting Solutions*
> Palo Alto, California

"Having been a psychologist and divorce educator myself for 25 years, I say without reservation that this new book is state of the art. It is not only easy to read but presented in such a way to make it easy to focus on points essential to parents living apart. Think of it as a DMV manual: a guide to steer parents from crashing their family units into hazards dangerous to themselves and their children. A must read!"

— P. Leslie Herold, PhD
Founder and president, Solutions for Families
San Bernardino, California

"Dr. Chet Muklewicz, a leader in divorce education, has done it again! With his wealth of experience and insight into the needs of separating and divorcing parents, this book covers many of the concerns and issues separating and divorcing parents face in a user-friendly way for parents to learn strategies and methods for child-centered communication, cooperation, and problem-solving. This wonderful resource can help parents help themselves and their children create a hopeful future and a healthy two-home family system."

— Eileen McCarten, MS, LCPC
Therapist, mediator, and parent educator, Family Matters-PACT
Rockford, Illinois

"Those of us who work with conflict and post-breakup families greatly appreciate the tools that are being offered in this book. All too often parents who are separated are unable to make joint decisions; however, this workbook really provides guidance and specific advice on how to think about and approach problem-solving after mom and dad have separated. It will help parents, married or not, to build a functional framework and establish a strategy for cooperative co-parenting. The worksheets make it easy to put into regular practice. It is a great resource for parents and professionals."

— Larry V. Swall, JD
Attorney and mediator
Liberty, Missouri

"I found this book to be helpful because there are a lot of things that I learned to do to help my baby deal with her parents being separated as she grows. I really liked the worksheets throughout the book to help break down each lesson."

— L.B. Mother of two children, one boy and one girl
Scranton, Pennsylvania

SAFEGUARDING
THE WELL-BEING OF CHILDREN DURING & AFTER A PARENTAL BREAKUP

An Evidence-Based Workbook for
Separating & Divorcing Parents to Ensure
the Healthy Adjustment of Their Children

by
Chet Muklewicz, EDD

Part I:
Fifty Years of Research
Identifies what helps and hinders
children as they cope with
parental breakups

Part II:
Family Transition Plan
Fifteen positive steps parents
can take to ensure the healthy
adjustment of their children

ISBN: 978-0-9704707-1-3
Chet Muklewicz, EDD
Printed in the United States of America

www.kidsfirst.cc

About the Author

Dr. Chet Muklewicz has twenty-five years of specialized experience acquired as a parent divorce educator, a trainer to legal and mental health professionals throughout the United States, a licensed psychologist specializing in children of divorce, and an author. Dr. Muklewicz developed a parent divorce education program called *Kids First* that he has personally presented to over 25,000 parents. He maintains a private practice providing individual and family therapy, serving several thousand families. In his clinical practice, he provides adjustment therapy to children and parents, parent coaching, co-parenting counseling, parent-child relationship therapy, and reunification therapy. He is frequently called upon to serve as an expert witness on child custody matters in Family Courts throughout Northeast Pennsylvania. He was a former Vice President, Academic Dean, and Professor of Psychology at Lackawanna College, and an adjunct Graduate School Lecturer in the Department of Counseling & Psychology at Marywood University—both in Scranton, Pennsylvania. He received his doctorate from Temple University and a post-doctoral certificate in family therapy training from the Philadelphia Child Guidance Center, University of Pennsylvania.

Limitations of this Guide

The information and guidance presented in this publication is built on a foundation of social science research that has proven to be relatively consistent over time. That said, the reader is reminded that this evidence-based guidance is limited to the reliability of the evidence itself. This guide is an educational resource meant to help parents make informed decisions as they navigate their way through family changes. The author recognizes that parental breakups are complex problems with interpersonal and situational dynamics unique to each family. There is no one-size-fits-all solution. For example, parents should cautiously consider this guidance where there is risk for domestic violence. The author does not claim that this information and guidance is complete or applicable to every situation and does not assume and hereby disclaims any liability to any person for any loss or damage caused by errors, inaccuracies, or omissions that may appear in this guide. This guide should not be used as a substitute for therapeutic support from mental health professionals. Users of this guide are solely responsible for determining the applicability of any information contained in this guide to their situations.

Series of Mini Videos

The author invites readers to view his

Kids First Parent Divorce Education Videos

free of charge

www.kidsfirst.cc

Snap Read

Review italicized highlights for a quick read

A Pennsylvania-Based Organization

Kids First Divorce Education Resources is located in Scranton, Pennsylvania.
It is not part of or affiliated with any other business or program registered
in any other state that includes, in part or in whole, the name Kids First.

Table of Contents

Foreword

I have had the privilege of serving as a judge in the Commonwealth of Pennsylvania for thirty-three years, spending twenty-four of those years presiding over a very busy Family Court. During my years on the bench, I have had an up-close view of parents going through the painful process of a family breakup. Many parents hold it together quite well and remain child-centered throughout the process. Children of these parents are very fortunate. Other children are not so lucky, as some parents are so unstable, conflicted, or stressed out that they do things that hurt their children and they are not even aware of it. What is most painful to see are children who suffer long-term emotional injuries caused by one or both parents who are more focused on their ex-partners then they are on their children. It is particularly difficult for judges because we know litigation alone cannot solve interparent relationship problems. Only parents can do that!

When I first became a Family Court judge, I was contemplating the start of a parent divorce education program for our Court system. At about that time, I received a letter from Dr. Muklewicz seeking to start the very same program I was hoping to introduce. The initial "Kids First Class" was presented in our county in 1996 and it continues today. Well over 25,000 parents have attended this program. It gives me great pleasure to introduce this book to parents and professionals as a wonderful resource that can guide parents through these troubling times. Dr. Muklewicz provides parents with poignant suggestions on how to ease the pain and suggests alternative approaches to resolving conflict. He has condensed decades of research and formulated a positive family transition plan in this user-friendly workbook. Parents, as well as legal and mental health professionals, will benefit from the guidance provided in this book. Most importantly, it will, as the title suggests, help to safeguard the well-being of children during and after a parental breakup.

Chester T. Harhut
Retired Judge, Court of Common Pleas, Lackawanna County, Pennsylvania

Introduction

An Evidence-Based Workbook for
Separating and Divorcing Parents
to Ensure the Healthy Adjustment of Their Children

Most separating parents worry about how their children will cope with their breakups. Will the children be okay? What can be done to help them? What is known about that? The short answer is that *there is a lot known about how children cope with and are affected by parental breakups.* Over five decades of research on the impact of divorce on children offers useful guidance on how parents can help children cope with family breakups. This guide, and the planning workbook contained within it, presents evidence-based guidance for parents to protect and promote the well-being of their children as they reorganize their family lives into two-home households. Grandparents and other family members who have been legally granted some degree of custody of children will find this guide useful as well.

Parental breakups launch children onto a journey of change. Those changes, such as getting used to living in two homes and grieving the loss of the family as it was previously known, require challenging adjustments for children. They are big changes and adapting to them will likely be stressful to children. How stressed will they be? Research tells us that there is great variability in the degree to which children are stressed by parental breakups—ranging from mild to crisis levels of stress. How long will they be stressed? *Most children are likely to at least experience temporary periods of stress* as their families transition into their new lives. Assuming family life eventually settles down, parents can expect it to take a year or two for children to substantially accommodate to their family changes. Research suggests children's adjustment to divorce has eased a bit over the decades, as it has become more normal in our culture. That said, even today, *a smaller but significant number of children will remain chronically stressed* and seriously symptomatic for years to come, potentially compromising their adult lives.

What kinds of stress-related problems can parents expect to see in their children? Overall, studies showed that children of divorce, when compared to children living with continuously married parents, were more likely to have emotional, behavioral, academic, and relationship problems. Age seems to influence the types of problems experienced by children. See the sections on "Common Age-Related Adjustment Problems." For most children, these problems will be transitional. For others, they will become chronic.

Why are some children more at risk than others? The adverse effects associated with parental breakups seem to be less about the children and more about their family situations. Those who get hurt and those who don't share similar sets of challenging changes: Both groups must adjust to their parents separating, start living out of two homes, and possibly join new schools and communities. Although these are significant changes, most children eventually adjust to them. Beyond those baseline changes, however, adversely affected children inescapably endure their *lives being comanaged by parents who cannot, and sometimes refuse to, work together* for their children. Their reactivity to each other eclipses and displaces the needs of their children. Children become centerpieces of parental conflict, sometimes driven by the instability of one or both parents. These unfortunate children are subject to intense and prolonged family instability and, consequently, are at greater risk. It should be noted that common adjustment problems, expected to be temporary, can become severe and chronic when co-parenting is compromised by intense interparent conflict. High-conflict parents are advised to review the sections on "Managing Safety Issues" and "Disengaging from Parent Conflict."

This book has been written on a premise of *hope*: There are, in fact, many healthy two-home families where children have not only survived parental breakups, they have gone on to thrive in their own lives. All families have a healthy version of themselves in post-separation family life. Even highly conflicted parents have the capability of separately *giving their children what they most need: a conflict-free homelife and a close relationship with a well-adjusted and attentive parent.*

PART I
Fifty Years of Research
Building Healthy Two-Home Families
on a Foundation of Evidence-Based Guidance

The study of the impact of parental breakups on children began with the rise of divorce rates in the 1970s. Since then there is some *fifty years of cumulative research offering insight into the challenges and circumstances that help and hinder the ability of children to make positive adjustments* to their family changes. The landscape of family life has significantly changed over the past half century. Most notably, many children in the United States are born to cohabitating parents who were never married. Consequently, this writing frequently refers to parental breakups instead of divorces. These research findings are meant to serve as a foundation of evidence-based guidance allowing parents to make informed decisions as they restructure their family lives.

Highlights of research are presented in a parent-friendly format allowing for meaningful application to family planning. The sections include effects of parental breakups on children, risk factors for children getting hurt, factors that protect children from harm, hope for children through parental empowerment, common age-related adjustment problems, and the impact of high-conflict parents. The author adds information drawn from his clinical experience into the narratives and are identified as "Likely observations." The primary research resources used in this writing are listed for the reader. Many of the resources provide reviews of research findings from the previous decade. *The Family Transition Plan Workbook listed in Part II presents fifteen parenting goals built on the foundation of this evidence-based guidance.*

Effects of Parental Breakups on Children

The impact of parental breakups on children has been studied for some fifty years. Each year, studies are published in dozens of professional peer-reviewed journals. Individual studies have been summarized in comprehensive impact reviews in the United States and other countries. The well-being impact profiles of children have proven to be rather consistent over time, suggesting a good measure of reliability of the information.

Impact of Parental Breakups on Children

Research reported that *children of divorce were found to have more behavioral, psychological, academic, and relationship problems* when compared to children living with non-separated married parents. Collectively, children of divorce had twice as many of those problems compared to children who remained in intact families. There were differences in how seriously children were affected by these problems and how long they lasted. In other words, not all children were affected in the same way. For most children, these problems were transitional. For a smaller percentage of children, they became chronic and long lasting.

Behavior Problems

Behavior problems included *oppositional, defiant, and acting out behaviors*. They occurred when children externalized their inner tensions outwardly toward others. Likely observations: Younger children might hit, hurt, or say mean things to parents and siblings. These behaviors are frequently seen after children transition from one parent to the other. Behavior problems in older children often include failing to follow rules and becoming disrespectful toward parents. Adolescent children might begin to defy authority figures at school or break societal rules in the community.

Psychological Adjustment Problems

Psychological problems included *anxiety, depression, anger, low self-esteem, and impaired social competence*. Likely observations: Most children will experience some measure of grief during and after the breakup. Their grief might be expressed as sadness, anger, or withdrawal from enjoyed activities. Internalizing behaviors might include worry, fearfulness, self-doubt, and social withdrawal. Young children may struggle with loyalty conflicts as they love parents upset with each other. Adolescent children dealing with loyalty conflict are more inclined to take sides.

School and Community Problems

It was reported that academic achievement of children of divorce was negatively affected by parental breakups. They tended to get *lower school grades and lower scores on standardized tests*. Adolescent children were more likely to skip or quit school before graduating. Likely observations: Children might be less prepared for their daily schoolwork and have difficulty paying attention or sitting still in school. Children with special needs may not have the coordinated parental support they need for success. Without it, they may have difficulty in meeting the demands of entering daycare, starting school, or participating in organized sports. They may have peer problems at school and in the community.

Relationship Losses

Research findings noted that parental breakups sometimes resulted in a *loss or diminished quality of relationship between children and their non-custodial parents*, usually their fathers. Studies of adult children of divorce reported that they regretted not having more custody time with their non-custodial parent, again usually their fathers. Children also lost contact or had diminished contact with other important people in their lives, including grandparents, extended family members, friends, and peers at school and in the community.

Problems May Persist into Adulthood

Studies reported that *adult children of divorce had lowered psychological well-being* and more adjustment problems. As adults, the quality of their lives were diminished because they had less education, lower job status, lower standard of living, and lower marital status than people who grew up in intact families. *They were more likely to get divorced themselves.* Likely observations: Reduced economic resources will limit opportunities for college or career training, which will limit their adult earning power. As adults, they may struggle in their own search for love, intimacy, and commitment. Aware of their parents' relationship, they may be fearful of marriage.

Risk Factors for Children Getting Hurt

The research reported that the negative effects associated with parental breakups are mostly due to family and other situational stressors. This section highlights those stressors, as well as characteristics of children that make them vulnerable.

Poor Parental Adjustment

Poorly adjusted parents were found to be chronically overwhelmed with anxiety, depression, or anger. This, in turn, impaired parenting by causing them to become agitated, overly punitive, and emotionally unavailable to their children. Likely observations: Parents with pre-existing adjustment problems are likely to be even more challenged by the stress of breakups. Serious mental health disorders or addiction to drugs or alcohol in one or both parents can create significant instability.

High Parental Conflict

Having highly conflicted parents has been identified as an important risk factor. Likely observations: Poorly adjusted parents will be highly reactive to conflict. *Parent conflict seen during breakups may be expressions of underlying histories of relationship and family instability* that existed long before the breakup and may continue after the breakup. Without some therapeutic or legal intervention, separation may not be enough to transform or end their conflict.

Children in the Middle

Exposure to intense and frequent parental conflict was reported to be stressful to children. Likely observations: High-conflict parents with long histories of family instability are likely to have pulled children into their conflict in years past and may be prone to doing so again in the future. They may have little insight to how their hurtful interactions affect their children, as these behaviors have become normalized over time. *The more intense and frequent the conflict between parents, the more significant the risk to children.*

Not Ready for New Partners

Introducing new partners to children before they are ready to handle it was reported as a significant risk factor. Research has reported some children found that parents taking on new partners was just as stressful as the parental breakup itself. Children were adversely affected by having multiple new partners join and subsequently leave their families. Likely observations: Most children will hold onto fantasies of their parents getting back together. Consequently, *they will lag behind parents in their readiness for new parental partners.* Older children may become oppositional to new partners who take on roles of authority. Children are likely to feel a stronger sense of kinship with new half-sibling than they are with new stepsiblings.

Economic Hardship

Income instability was found to have negative consequences for children. Likely observations: Money problems may pressure parents into cohabitating with new partners. Child and spousal support problems can force unwanted lifestyle changes, such as dropping out of desired activities.

Individual Child Vulnerability

Some children were found to be more at risk because of unique *vulnerabilities, including those who were highly sensitive, had poorly developed coping skills, or had disorders* that compromised their ability to make healthy adjustments. The ages of children were found to predispose them to problems unique to their developmental stages.

Stress Overload

Parental breakups have been conceptualized as family crises that stress children with short-term challenges. In this model children will be affected by the number and intensity of the challenges triggered by the breakup. In time, most children find relief as they adjust to their post-separation families. A second model expands the view of how children are stressed by parental separations. From this perspective *children are stressed by an accumulation of chronic risk factors* that increase and prolong parental and family instability. These might include children having one or two poorly adjusted parents, long histories of parental and family instability, ongoing parental conflict, introduction of multiple new partners, chronic litigation, and income instability—to name some but not all. Combinations of acute and chronic stressors can overwhelm children.

Factors that Protect Children from Harm

The research identified a list of protective factors that shield children from harm and advance their well-being. This section highlights those helpful situational factors.

What Are Protective Factors?

Researchers have used a stress adjustment model to describe the situational dynamics that predict whether children will be adversely affected by parental breakups. In this model, the final outcomes are influenced by a mix of risk and protective factors. Risk factors increase the likelihood of children getting hurt. Those were presented in a previous section. *The protective factors presented in this section are associated with healthy outcomes for children.*

Parental Stability and Adjustment

One of the best predictors of the well-being of children was when children had a close emotional relationship with at least one stable, well-adjusted parent. These parents were found to have hopeful attitudes toward the future. Likely observations: Despite the challenges of coping with breakups, *healthy parents will be able to remain child-centered and emotionally available to children*. They are likely to be resilient, have good coping skills, and can adjust to separations.

Cooperative Co-parenting

Children did better when parents were able to remain child-centered and cooperative in their childcare efforts. Co-parenting counseling or coordination services helped high-conflict parents to work together on parenting while maintaining appropriate interpersonal boundaries. These services are sometimes ordered by the Court.

Keeping Children Out of the Middle

Keeping children out of the middle of parental conflict was significantly associated with positive outcomes for children. The adverse effects associated with parental breakups were found to be minimized when parents were able to encapsulate or shield children from their conflicted interactions. Likely observations: *One conflict-free home can function as an island of stability and respite for children*. For some children, these safe places might be found in the homes of grandparents or extended family members.

Authoritative Parenting Style

Researchers found that children benefited when either or both parents used an authoritative approach to parenting. This involves a blend of *holding children to expectations while engaging them in an encouraging and sensitive manner.*

Patience in Introducing New Partners

Studies reported that children did better when parents *gave them adequate time to adjust to the breakup before introducing new partners*. Likely observations: Such parents are able to see that their own readiness for a new partner exceeds the readiness of their children. When they introduce new partners, they do it in slow, incremental steps.

Economic Stability

Research suggested that children benefited when parents avoided or at least minimized the instability caused by the reduction of financial resources that occurs with parental breakups. *Even when there is a drop in income, it helps when the ability to meet basic needs can be stabilized.*

Tolerable Stress Demand

Children were found to do best if parents were able to *limit the amount of stress and change children had to endure*. Parents are advised to review the section on "Seeing Problems Through the Eyes of a Child" so they can make necessary changes without overwhelming the children.

Coping Skills of Children

Some children were found to have *social and coping skills that improved their ability to adjust* to parental breakups. Likely observation: Children will benefit from strengthening their coping skills.

Supportive Resources

Researchers also reported that parents and children *benefited from social support of friends, extended family, coworkers, and classmates*. Support from therapists, school programs, divorce education programs, and mediation have also proven to be helpful.

Hope for Children Through Parental Empowerment

The research has identified lists of risk and protective factors that can be used by parents to protect and promote the well-being of children.

Evidence for Hope

Researchers indicated that most children from divorced families (75–80 percent) were found to be in the "normal" range when assessed for psychological adjustment. Parents should take some comfort in knowing that most children will eventually adjust and accommodate to changes in their families. Evidence suggests that, within a year or two, children will likely accept how their families have changed. Further, there is *evidence of children moving on to thrive in their post-separation lives. These findings represent a message of hope.*

Reason for Concern

While there is evidence inspiring hope, there are findings that arouse worry as well. Decades of research has consistently reported that children of divorce had *more emotional, behavioral, academic, and relationship problems* than children from intact families. Some research has suggested that as many as one in five or six children might experience varying degrees of adjustment problems, some of which might extend into their adult lives. *Clearly a message of worry.*

Pursue Hope and Avoid Risk

Breakups set families on courses of change likely to trigger grief and stress reactions in parents and children. Parents are encouraged to pause, pivot, and contemplate a hopeful future where children are likely to adjust and ultimately enjoy their redesigned families. At the same time, evidence warning that children may be adversely affected should not be ignored or dismissed. Rather this evidence should be used to plan the journey from the present to the future. It should be anticipated that some risk and jeopardy may be encountered along the way. Research indicates that the potential risks to be found on their journeys are largely known and can be avoided or mitigated. Armed with good information, *parents can take responsible steps to shield their children from potential harm as they pursue hopeful family outcomes* where children will be loved and cared for by both parents.

Situational Relief

Historically, counseling methods to help children with adjustment problems focused on changing the children themselves. Problems and solutions were understood to be within the children. The *Family Systems* approach expanded this view. Adjustment problems of children are then seen as expressions of dysfunctional family dynamics. For example, children will be stressed when parents displace anger on them or when parents put them in the middle of their conflict. From this perspective, *problems and solutions are situational.* Relief is achieved by making situational changes.

Parental Empowerment

Using the stress adjustment model, researchers identified two critically important lists of situational factors that will either jeopardize or protect the well-being of children. Evidence-based research on risk factors can empower parents to make informed decisions to avoid acting in ways that will jeopardize the well-being of their children. It also provides evidence-based information on protective factors that will *empower parents to take positive steps to enhance the well-being of their children.*

Power of One Parent Can Be Good Enough

Separating parents worried about the well-being of their children are often mutually frustrated by their inability to influence each other to see things their way. It is a frustration that leads to a sense of powerlessness. Parents should shift their efforts into doing what is in their control and, barring imminent safety issues, accept and let go of what they cannot control. *Either parent has the potential to give their children a substantial dose of what they most need: At least one conflict-free home and a close relationship with a stable and well-ad-*

justed parent. Doing so may not always produce ideal or perfect family situations, but it may give children enough of what they need to make healthy adjustments. The parenting workbook in the next section will guide parents to work individually or collaboratively toward that end.

Primary Research Resources

Amato, P.R. (2000). The consequences of divorce for adults and children. *Journal of Marriage & Family*, 62, 1296-1287.

Amato, P.R. (2010). Research on divorce: Continuing trends and new developments. *Journal of Marriage & Family*, 72 (3), 650-666.

Babb, B.A & Kline Pruett, M. Eds. (2020). Special Issue: Parent-Child Contact Problems: Concepts, Controversies, Conundrums. Family Court Review, 58 (2).

Baude, A., Pearson, J., & Drapeau, S. (2016). Child adjustment in joint physical custody versus sole custody: A meta-analytic review. *Journal of Divorce and Remarriage*, 57 (5), 338-360.

Cavanagh, S.E. & Huston, A.C. (2006). Family instability and children's early problem behavior. *Social Forces*, 85, 551–581.

Kelly, J.B. (2000). Children's adjustment in conflicted marriage and divorce: A decade review of research. *Child & Adolescent Psychiatry*, 39, 963–973.

Kelly, J. B. (2007). Children's living arrangements following separation and divorce: Insights from empirical and clinical research. *Family Process*, 46, 35–52.

Kelly, J. B. (2012). Risk and protective factors associated with child and adolescent adjustment following separation and divorce: Social science applications. In K. Kuehnle & L. Drozd (Eds.), *Parenting plan evaluations: Applied research for the family court* (p. 49–84). Oxford University Press.

Manning, W.D. (2015). Cohabitation and child well-being. *Future Child*, 25 (2), 51-66.

Raley, R.K. & Sweeney, M.M. (2020). Divorce, repartnering, and stepfamilies: A decade in Review. *Journal of Marriage & Family*, 82, 81-99.

Parental Assessment of Risk to Children

Have Your Children Been Exposed to These Risk Factors?

Directions: Write how each parent may have exposed children to these risk factors.

Children Living with a Poorly Adjusted Parent

Mom: _____

Dad: _____

Children Witnessing Interparent Conflict

Mom: _____

Dad: _____

Children Put in the Middle of Parent Conflict

Mom: _____

Dad: _____

Introduction of a Parent's New Partner Before Children are Ready (1–2 years)

Mom: _____

Dad: _____

Children Losing Contact with a Parent & Significant Others

Mom: _____

Dad: _____

Children Exposed to Economic Hardship and Financial Instability

Mom: _____

Dad: _____

Children Having Poor Coping Skills

Mom: _____

Dad: _____

Children Having Too Many Life Changes and Challenges

Mom: _____

Dad: _____

Common Age-Related Adjustment Problems

This section presents common age-related adjustment problems. They may be temporary and transitional, or they may become serious and chronic when co-parenting is compromised by intense interparent conflict.

Infants and Toddlers
Newborns to 2.5 Years of Age

Sleep Problems

After her parents separated, this 18-month-old little girl lived with one parent five nights a week and spent two nights a week with the other parent. While in the care of the parent who had her for five nights, she was routinely put to bed at 8 p.m. and would wake up at 7 a.m. the next morning. At the other home, there was no regular bedtime schedule. She might stay up as late as 11 p.m. When she was returned to the parent who had her five nights, it would take that parent two or three days to get the child back into her regular sleep schedule. During that time, she was irritable, agitated, and did not take afternoon naps. Her parents did not speak to each other and could not resolve her sleep problems. This child's irritability was a direct product of parental conflict.

What children need: *It is clearly understood that young children will benefit and likely thrive when their parents mutually support a stable sleep routine.* This would include a shared bedtime, as well as a shared schedule for napping. Having a shared bedtime routine would further help children adjust to living in two homes. For example, both parents might have a shared routine starting with a bath at 7 p.m., followed by a snack, then a bedtime reading, and finally tucking in at 8 p.m.

Separation Anxiety

It was time for a two-year-old boy to transition from one parent to the other. The exchange occurred on the front porch. It was an emotionally intense moment. One parent rang the doorbell and the other opened the door. The parents glared at each other without speaking. One uttered a sarcastic remark and an argument ensued. When it was time to exchange the child, the little boy began to cry, as he clung desperately to the delivering parent saying, "No, no, no!!" The delivering parent said, "He doesn't want to be with you!" The receiving parent said, "You are turning him against me!" The delivering parent said, "I'm taking him back home," and walked away. The receiving parent said, "I'm calling my attorney!" This child's distress was an expression of parent conflict.

What children need: Children at this young age are forming attachment bonds to both parents. Children will feel most secure when they are emotionally connected or "attached" to their caregivers. *It is normal for children of this age to cling as they disconnect from one parent and reconnect to the other.* In these moments of transition, parents should intentionally bring a calm demeanor, avoid provocative comments or reactions, avoid emotionally intense goodbyes, and purposefully let the child witness civility.

Abandonment Reactions

A two-year-old girl was strongly attached to both of her parents. For reasons she could not understand, she had lost contact with one of her parents. With one parent gone, she began to hyper-cling to the only parent still available to her. She was worried that her remaining parent might disappear as well. She became anxious and insecure. Parental conflict is associated with children losing contact with a parent and other involved caretakers.

What children need: *They need to be reassured that the loved ones in their lives will remain in their lives.* Intellectual explanations will not suffice. They need routine contact with their loved ones, including grandparents and extended family.

Preschool Children
Three to Five Years of Age

Self-blame

A five-year-old boy woke one morning to discover that one of his parents had left the home and was not coming back. He then remembered that the parent who left had yelled at him the night before for not picking up his toys. He became very sullen and distraught. His parents had no idea that he had come to believe that he was to blame for their breakup. Most parents would not imagine that their children would ever come to such unlikely conclusions. The impact of self-blaming thoughts can leave children with a potentially painful message imprinted on their self-identities: "I did something bad. My mom or dad left me and doesn't want me anymore." These self-blaming beliefs can become a lens for viewing other relationships as well. The boy mentioned above stopped playing a sport he liked because he believed the kids on the team "didn't like me anymore." He then started saying that the kids at school didn't like him either. He became quick to perceive rejection by others.

Children this age have a unique quality of self-referenced thinking that makes them vulnerable to blaming themselves for parental breakups. This self-referenced thinking is the same thought process that guides them in selecting childlike gifts for parents, such as dolls or action figures. They use themselves to explain the world around them, including the reason why parents have separated.

What children need: These children are not likely to describe or explain their self-blaming thoughts. However, if parents ask them if they have ever had such thoughts, they are likely to acknowledge them. Doing so will give parents an opportunity to correct these disturbing thoughts. *Parents should explicitly tell their children they did not cause the breakup.* Further, they should be mindful not to argue in front of the children.

Acting-out Behavior

One morning, at an exchange, mom and dad had gotten into a huge argument. It lasted for about ten minutes and their son was right in the middle of it. The argument was loud and quite disturbing. Dad eventually left with his son, dropped the boy off at preschool, and then was off to work. An hour later, dad received a phone call from the school stating that his son had been biting other children and his father had to take the boy home. The teacher told the dad that the school had a policy that biting would not be tolerated, and the boy had to leave school for the day.

The father then picked up his son from school. On the ride home, dad was upset and sternly asked his son, "Why were you biting children at school?" The boy responded, "I don't know." The boy was right, he didn't know. He was disturbed by the parental fighting, but he did not have the skills to put those feelings into words. Instead, he acted out his feelings by biting children at school. Parents are often perplexed by extreme tantrums of their preschoolers, especially when they transition from one parent to the other. Acting out behavior might include hitting siblings, parents, or pets. They might even break their own toys. *Although they may not understand parental conflict, they will surely feel it.* Overwhelmed with emotion, these children will be inclined to act out their feelings.

What children need: Parents need to be mindful of the presence of their children when they argue. Keep in mind that many children are exposed to conflict by overhearing phone conversations. *Generally, at this age, if children do not see or hear the conflict, they are not likely to be affected by it.* Help preschool children learn to express their feelings with words rather than acting out behavior. See the section on "Helping Children Express Their Feelings with Words."

Early Elementary School Children
Six to Eight Years of Age

School Problems

A seven-year-old boy was in second grade. In the care of one parent the night before, he was taken to school the next morning and was later picked up by the other parent after school. He was crying when the receiving parent picked him up from school. "What's wrong buddy?" asked the receiving parent. The child went on to explain that he was embarrassed because he arrived late for school, did not have his homework completed, and did not know he had a spelling test that day. He failed the spelling test and received a zero as a homework grade. Since his parents did not speak to each other, this boy did not have the coordinated parental support he needed to be successful. His poor grades and his painful emotional reaction were a direct result of parental conflict.

Educational research tells us that children will form an identity as a learner by the time they complete the third grade. Children will form ideas about liking or disliking school based on the emotional satisfaction of day-to-day school experiences. If the boy in the example cited above were to experience frequent frustration, he will likely define himself as someone who does not like school. This negative school identity will likely set him off on a course of avoidance. He may gravitate to school peers who share negative views of school. Such unfortunate children are likely to have many bad school days ahead of them.

What children need: These young children need both parents to be well informed about school, get to know teachers and school staff members, support and coach their children's learning activities, and get the children to school on time. *Children who have co-parent academic support have a far better chance of liking school and becoming achievement oriented.*

Loyalty Conflicts

An eight-year-old boy was about to be exchanged from one parent to the other. Just before he left his mom's home, his mother said to him, "I have to ask you an important question because we are going to Court on Monday." She asked, "Would you prefer to live mostly with me or mostly with your father?" The boy's eyes opened wide and he faintly whispered, "You." "Ok, thanks," she said. Just a few minutes later, he got in his father's car, and his father asked him the same question: "Would you prefer to live mostly with me or mostly with your mother?" Again, in a cautious tone he said to his father, "You." Now both parents, each armed with the endorsement of their son, were ready to fight the good fight to give their son what he wanted.

Another example: As a little girl was transitioning from one parent to the other, she said to the parent she was leaving that she hated the other parent's new partner, saying, "I don't want to spend time with that person." The little girl was reassured by the sending parent that the matter would be taken care of. Then she got in the car with the receiving parent and, upon realizing that the new partner was not there, she asked where this person was and said that she was "looking forward to spending time" with this person. As these children grow in awareness of parental feelings, they become exceedingly stressed by painful loyalty conflicts: To love one parent becomes an act of disloyalty to the other parent. *They may hide their love for one parent while in the care of the other parent.*

What children need: *Parents should give children permission to love and be loved by the other parent.* Parents should consider negative reports made by children about the other parent may be exaggerations made to please the listener.

Understanding the Dynamics of Loyalty Conflicts

Anxiety of Loyalty Conflicts

The soccer game was over. Our team won! Yeah! Then, the child turned to see his mon and dad standing on opposite sides of the field, each waving for him to come over. What to do? Should he go to mom? Go to dad? Not knowing what to do, he stopped and started tying and retying his shoes. Developmentally, this child was acutely aware that his conflicted parents did not get along. *To go to one would risk hurting the feelings of the other. Making such choices force children into what will feel like acts of disloyalty to the parent not chosen.* It starts with anxiety and ends with guilt.

A child was talking on the phone to one parent in front of the other disapproving parent. The child became stiff giving yes or no answers. "What's wrong?" the parent asked. "Nothing," replied the child. Another example: picking a sport to play when each parent wanted their son to play a different sport created anxiety. Each parent privately asked, "What sport do you want to play?" The boy told his mom he wanted to play the sport she wanted him to play and he told his dad he wanted to play the sport he wanted him to play. It was not about picking a sport. He had to pick a parent!

Mirroring Parental Views is a Way of Relieving Anxiety in the Moment

Parents might not recognize their own child when in the care of the other parent. A fifteen-year-old girl was to start high school in a few months. She was a good student. One parent wanted her to go to a prep school nearby. The other wanted her to go to the regional public school, which also was a good school. The parents did not speak to each other. The child told the parent who wanted her to attend the prep school that she wanted to go to the prep school. This child then told the other parent that she wanted to go to the regional public school supported by that parent. *This girl had tee shirts of both schools and she would wear the "correct" tee shirt for each parent. The child's behavior was her best effort to cope with an unbearable situation.* But it only made things worse. Each parent was validated by what she told them. They litigated the issue and sought Court approval of their preferences. The girl cried when she had to testify in Court.

Late Elementary School Children
Nine to Twelve Years of Age

 Identity Problems

This is a story of a ten-year-old boy. His parents had been divorced for five years. Neither separation nor time had softened the conflict between his parents. Over the years, he learned to quiet his anxiety by concealing his feelings for each parent when in the presence of the other parent. He was too scared to tell the truth: that he loved the person that each parent hated. As he became good at mirroring the feelings of an upset parent, he slowly lost touch with his own feelings, his own truths. *It was a bit of a role reversal. His parents should*

have been validating his truths and feelings. Instead, his parents relied on him to validate their truths and feelings.

Each parent routinely criticized the other parent to this boy. Once he got mad when one of his parents criticized the other to him. He got scolded for acting like "a Smith again," the surname of the other parent. Not surprisingly, he regressed to hiding his feelings again. The tensions of high-conflict parents have an arresting effect on the development of self-identity. Soon this boy will be entering middle school with a coping style of hiding his own feelings and deferring to the opinions and feelings of others. His poorly defined sense of self will create many challenges for him.

What children need: Self-identity develops into an inner guidance system for children: A core set of personal beliefs, values, and feelings that define them as individuals. Making good life decisions requires knowing who you are, what you value, what you like, whom you trust, and what is right and wrong, just to name a few. This inner self-definition develops over time. *Children need parents to encourage and validate their efforts of "trying out" ideas of themselves.* Parental displays of mutual civility and respect give children instructive guidance on how to treat other people.

Taking Sides

Children of this age do not yet have the skills to fully understand or resolve complex relationship problems. Consequently, *these children are prone to dealing with their conflicted feelings by taking sides with one parent against the other parent.* It is an age when they are very inquisitive and, therefore, are not likely to miss much of the conflict going on between their parents. There are different degrees of alignment with a parent. In a mild form, they can be chronically annoyed with the disfavored parent. In moderate alignments, they might be angry and disrespectful while still spending time with the disliked parent. In extreme forms, they might fully refuse to speak to or spend any time with one of their parents.

There is a continuum of reasons why children reject parents. At one end, we see parents doing things that disturb or offend children, such as violent, criminal, drug addiction, or emotionally abusive behavior. In such cases, children's avoidant behavior is understandable and normal. At the other end of the continuum, children reject parents because of extreme alignment with prejudices of their favored parents. Interparent conflict sets the stage for this rejecting behavior. Children who have been successfully manipulated to reject a parent without substantial cause for doing so are considered to be alienated. In most cases, children are influenced by the actions of favored parents and the reactions of rejected parents.

What children need: These children need their parents to set a strict boundary that keeps them out of their adult issues. Parents need to help children to appreciate the complexities of the family breakup. *Help them to learn skills to solve relationship problems rather than abandoning a parent.* Court-appointed therapeutic help may be needed to facilitate reunification.

Adolescent Children
Thirteen to Eighteen Years of Age

Risky Behavior

Despite their strained relationship, mom and dad were both proud of their fifteen-year-old son. He was an honor roll student, captain of the football team, and was a well-mannered young man. Although their son was aware that his parents fought a lot, he was not prepared for their abrupt separation that occurred when one parent walked out after an argument and never returned home. Nor was he prepared when the same parent moved in with a new partner shortly after. By the next school grading quarter, his grades dropped significantly, and he quit the football team. Then he started to get into trouble at school. He was suspended for vaping marijuana in the stairwell and suspended a second time for sending inappropriate pictures to a female student in his class. His parents wondered what was wrong with their son.

Discipline Problems

There were two brothers, one fourteen and the other twelve, who lived in a 50-50 shared custody arrangement. One summer afternoon, while in the care of one parent, both boys were asked by that parent to help with some yardwork. They both said okay but only the twelve-year-old went out to help. The fourteen-year-old boy stayed inside playing a video game. He was asked several times to come outside and help with the yardwork. Finally, on the fourth time, a very frustrated parent came in and yelled at the boy for ignoring the requests for help. The boy got angry and said, "I don't have to put up with this BS," left the house, and walked to the other parent's home that was a mile away. He then refused to return to the other parent. Nor would he take calls from that parent. His parents had very different parenting styles—the parent whom the boy returned to was soft on discipline and had few, if any, expectations around the house. The other parent was not overly strict but had reasonable expectations for the boy to help out with chores. The boy finally returned after Court-ordered reunification therapy.

Relationship Problems

A sixteen-year-old girl was the only child of two highly conflicted parents. She always felt closer to one parent and more distant from the other. Primary custody went to the preferred parent. When she spent time with the less preferred parent, she would typically go to her room and engage her friends on social media. She would take her meals to her room and almost completely avoid this parent. The rejected parent felt that the other parent overindulged and spoiled this child. As a result, this parent set out to correct this flaw in the child by becoming strict, demanding, and authoritative. Their relationship consisted of the parent demanding chores, the girl refusing, and her parent punishing her for not doing them.

What children need: When we think of grief, we normally think of sadness. However, *adolescent children may show their grief in a variety of ways.* Grief might be expressed as *anger or oppositional behavior,* such as the boy refusing to help with yardwork. Grief might be expressed in *social withdrawal,* such as the girl who withdrew to her bedroom when visiting a parent. Grief can manifest as *risky behavior,* such as the boy who got into trouble at school for vaping. Adolescence is a time of life when teens are often in conflict with their parents over wanting more independence and less parental supervision. The boy who walked out on his father refusing to visit him again is a situation that often happens with separated parents. Parents of adolescent children need to be aware of the issues experienced by adolescent children so they might avoid feeding into these problems. They need to work together to find child-centered values they can mutually support.

Impact of High-Conflict Parents:
Letters and Drawings from Children

The adjustment problems reviewed in this section are likely to be transitional for most children. However, children raised by high-conflict parents are at risk for these problems becoming chronic and long lasting.

Girl Resists Mommy Replacement

"At three years old, I was too young to understand about my parents' divorce. All I knew was that I had two of everything. Two houses. Two sets of toys. Everything that I wanted. This only lasted a couple of years. By the time I was nine or ten, I dreaded going over to my father's house because there was another woman there that my father tried to get me to call mommy. I became very angry because I already had a mother and didn't want a new one. My weekly visits turned into weekly fights."

Jennifer, age 22
Age 3 at the time of separation

Boy Loses Father

"I came home from school and found my mother crying in the kitchen. She said, 'Your father is gone and wants nothing to do with us.' I cried and ran to my room where I talked to no one for several days. One day my mother came into my room and said, 'The bastard is here and wants to talk to you. Go down and tell him to get lost.' I was so glad to see him, but I knew if I let go of that emotion my mother would have felt betrayed. So from that day on, I have never spoken to him."

Robert, age 19
Age 10 at the time of separation

A Child's Loyalty Dilemma

A seven-year-old girl drew this picture of her family. Her mother is on the left with a new baby and her father is on the right with a new wife. Both parents routinely quizzed her about her time spent with the other parent. They frequently litigated based on her reports. The vertical line between the two sides describes her loyalty dilemma. Asked why she did not draw herself in the picture she said, "I didn't know where to put myself."

Children Listen to Parental Fighting

This picture was drawn by a nine-year-old boy. He is the one on the left with tears coming out of his eyes. His young brother is on the other side with his hand cupping his ear, making the point that children will always be listening if they are within earshot. These boys were chronically exposed to parental arguments. Hearing their own names in the argument made them sad, scared, and worried that they might have been the cause of the fighting.

This picture was drawn by a nine-year-old girl. Her drawing is a graphic description of the pain many children feel when they are caught in the middle of parental conflict. Her tears are an expression of the intensity of her stress. Her cry for "Help!!" reminds us how powerless children are in this situation. Her portrayal of both parents yelling and pulling on her tells a story of how high-conflict parents fail to recognize how their actions can hurt their children.

This picture captures just one snapshot of a single moment of pain for this little girl. Actually, her story had a childhood filled with the same or similar pictures. Like many children situated in the middle of highly conflicted parents going through a relationship breakup, this child was at risk for developing short and long-term adjustment problems. In fact, she was being treated by her pediatrician for physical ailments and she was being seen by a counselor for an anxiety disorder.

Both powerless and stressed, all this child could do was to become symptomatic. And that only seemed to intensify the fighting between her parents, as each viewed their daughter's pain as being caused by the other parent. Consequently, each tried to relieve their daughter's pain by removing or limiting the other parent's access to the child. But each parent was unable to get rid of the other. So, the harder they tried to remove each other from the child's life, the more they increased the child's pain. This child was stuck in the middle of a toxic pattern of parental reactivity: The more she suffered, the more they fought. The more they fought, the more she suffered.

Like many children suffering the pain of parental conflict, this little girl was receiving medical treatment for her stress. This was not a sick or a disturbed child. She was a child suffering from a disturbing situation. In essence, she was being medicated because her parents could not get along! That would be like taking pain medication for having a stone in your shoe. Better to remove the stone! This child needed situational relief.

"When little people are overwhelmed by big emotions,
it's our job to share our calm, not join their chaos."

— L.R. Knost

— Single-Parent Worksheet —
Assessment of Child Adjustment Problems
One Parent's View of Child Adjustment Problems

This worksheet presents age-related adjustment problems that are commonly seen among children during parental breakups. These problems are likely to be temporary and transitional as families adjust and settle into their post-separation lives. They may become serious and chronic with long-term family instability. List the names of children in each age group and place a checkmark by the age-related adjustment problems they may be experiencing at this time. Add notes for clarification.

Infants and Toddlers (Birth to 2.5 Years of Age)   Names: _____
- ❑ Sleep problems: _____
- ❑ Separation anxiety: _____
- ❑ Abandonment reactions: _____
- ❑ Other problems: _____

Preschool Children (3 to 5 Years of Age)   Names: _____
- ❑ Self-blame: _____
- ❑ Acting-out: _____
- ❑ Other problems: _____

Early Elementary School Children (6 to 8 Years of Age) Names: _____
- ❑ School problems: _____
- ❑ Loyalty problems: _____
- ❑ Other problems: _____

Late Elementary School Children (9 to 12 Years of Age) Names: _____
- ❑ Identity problems: _____
- ❑ Taking sides: _____
- ❑ Other problems: _____

Adolescent Children (13 to 18 Years of Age) Names: _____
- ❑ Risky behavior: _____
- ❑ Relationship problems: _____
- ❑ Other problems: _____

PART II
Family Transition Plan
Fifteen positive steps parents can take to ensure the healthy adjustment of their children

How to Use This Parenting Workbook

Use It to Plan for a Healthy Post-Separation Two-Home Family
Parents should embrace the idea that there is a healthy version of themselves in post-separation family life. This plan outlines positive steps for them to achieve that end.

Each Parent Should Prepare an Individual Plan
After reviewing the content, checklists, and worksheets presented in each of the fifteen positive steps, parents should complete the "Individual Family Transition Plan" provided on page 30.

Parents Should Work Together on a Shared Plan
After preparing their individual plans, parents are encouraged to compare their completed plans and work together on a "Shared Family Transition Plan" provided at the end of this workbook.

Meet Nathan

Nathan is five years old. His parents are getting divorced. They are worried because Nathan has been very sad and has been acting out with temper tantrums.

Nathan's Situational Family Stress

The breakup of Nathan's parents has been very stressful for him. His adjustment will be significantly influenced by the number and intensity of the stressful challenges he must endure.

Nathan's Limited Ability to Cope

Nathan is only five years old. His coping skills are limited, and he is powerless to stop the unwanted changes in his family. His adjustment demands are beyond his ability to cope.

Family Transition Plan Strategies to Help Nathan

Reduce Initial & Transitional Family Stress	Improve Long-Term Family Stability	Increase Stress Tolerance & Resiliency
✔ Telling the Children ✔ Helping Children Express Feelings with Words ✔ Seeing Problems Through the Eyes of a Child ✔ Conflict-Free Exchanges of the Children ✔ Keeping Children Out of the Middle	✔ Vision of a Healthy Two-Home Family ✔ Parents Taking Care of Themselves ✔ Disengaging from Parent Conflict ✔ Resetting Parenting Boundaries ✔ Co-parenting Communication ✔ Cautiously Introducing New Partners	✔ Improving Coping Skills of Children ✔ Using an Authoritative Parenting Style ✔ Building Healthy Support Systems

— Single-Parent Worksheet —
Individual Family Transition Plan

One Parent's Plan to Help Children

This Family Transition Plan is built on a premise of hope: The well-being of children is best protected and promoted by having an optimal amount of stability in their post-separation lives. This plan includes fifteen parenting goals that have been crafted from the list of risk and protective factors obtained from the research. It is an aspirational plan designed to give children healthy two-home families in which they are likely to thrive in their lives. Completion of these goals will help to reduce short-term stress, improve long-term family stability, and build resiliency in children.

Rank the Level of Priority for Each Goal

Directions: Place one, two, or three checkmarks to indicate the priority for goal implementation:

1=Important Goal 2= Very Important Goal 3=Critically Important Goal

  ☑ ☑ ☑ Example of checkmarks for a critically important goal

— — — Vision of a healthy two-home family

— — — Parents taking care of themselves

— — — Disengaging from parent conflict

— — — Seeing problems through the eyes of a child

— — — Keeping children out of the middle

— — — Managing safety issues

— — — Telling the children

— — — Resetting parenting boundaries

— — — Co-parenting communication cautiously

— — — Introducing new partners

— — — Helping children express themselves with words

— — — Conflict-free exchanges of the children

— — — Improving coping skills of children

— — — Using an authoritative parenting style

— — — Building healthy support systems

Vision of a Healthy Two-Home Family

GOAL: For parents to describe a healthy two-home family where there is enough family stability for children to adjust and thrive in their lives

Breakups and the Big Question: Now What?

Parental breakups often flood families with stressful challenges, such as money problems, home relocation, new schools, and litigation over custody of the children, just to name a few. Parents are often overwhelmed by the volume and intensity of these adjustment demands. These demands and the potential of interparent conflict can leave parents stressed and highly focused on the current problems. The urgency of day-to-day concerns can keep parents stuck in crisis mode. *Parents should step back, look at the big picture, and ask, "Now what?"* Perhaps it is time to shift focus away from problems of the past and present and start looking for healthy outcomes in the future.

— Worksheet —

Pivoting Toward the Future

Not an End—A Time for Change

Over the course of a lifetime, most people will encounter at least a few major life events that will trigger the breaking apart of life as it was once known—leaving them facing a future of uncertainty and apprehension. Married or not, parental breakups rank high among life problems such as a serious chronic illness or the death of a family member. The grief following family breakups will keep everyone focused on its ending. Grief is necessary, but it is not the final destination. Grief can lead to acceptance which, in turn, can lead to a realization that it is a time to pivot toward the future. *A new family life lies ahead.*

Notes: _____

Healthy Two-Home Families Exist

It is important to recognize and appreciate that healthy two-home families do, in fact, exist. It is in these healthy two-home family environments that children are most likely to be well adjusted and thrive in their lives. Parents should consider that a vision of a healthy two-home family can be crafted even when there are imperfect situations and imperfect parents. In other words, *every family has a healthy version of themselves.* Parents who are looking for hope will have the best chance of finding it.

Notes: _____

Start with Shared Values for the Children

Even when parents are conflicted, they likely share similar child-centered values: Safeguarding their physical health and well-being, nurturing their emotional and behavioral health and well-being, encouraging their school achievement, promoting their social adjustment, and, of course, keeping them safe. Parental childcare functions should also be included: Interparent communication, conflict-free exchanges, and keeping children out of the middle of parental conflict. In the next section, parents are encouraged to use these child-centered values to write their own vision statements.

Shared values might include:

- ❏ Doing well in school
- ❏ Respectful behaviors
- ❏ Good work habits
- ❏ Trustworthiness
- ❏ Healthy habits
- ❏ Physical fitness
- ❏ Sport activities

- ❏ Good manners
- ❏ Responsibility
- ❏ Honesty
- ❏ Teamwork
- ❏ Helpful and cooperative
- ❏ Spiritual development
- ❏ Good routines

Notes: _____

— *Worksheet* —

Writing a Healthy Two-Home Family Vision Statement

Example of a Joint Vision Statement

As separating parents, we recognize that our children will need us to work cooperatively together now more than ever. Our goal is to establish a healthy two-home family where the children would be best able to thrive in their lives. We recognize that our own well-being is a foundation for the well-being of our children, and we commit to taking care of ourselves. We commit to raising our children with a list of shared values that include keeping them safe, encouraging them to do well in school, and nurturing their physical, social, and emotional development. Recognizing that we will be co-parents forever, we commit to shielding our children from parental conflict, sharing childcare information, and collaborating on decision-making and problem-solving. Finally, as parents we commit to giving our children a family legacy where they can be proud of their parents for putting them first.

Develop Your Own Vision Statement

To be written as: ___ A joint statement   ___ A single-parent statement   ___ Both

Describe your version of a healthy single- or two-home family: _____

_____

Make a statement about self-care: _____

_____

List critical childcare values (such as safety, school achievement, etc.): _____

_____

Make a statement about co-parenting functions: _____

_____

Make a statement about family legacy: _____

_____

Check Childcare Values You Can Mutually Support

- ❏ Doing well in school
- ❏ Respectful behaviors
- ❏ Good work habits
- ❏ Trustworthiness
- ❏ Healthy habits
- ❏ Physical fitness
- ❏ Sport activities

- ❏ Good manners
- ❏ Responsibility
- ❏ Honesty
- ❏ Teamwork
- ❏ Helpful and cooperative
- ❏ Spiritual development
- ❏ Good routines

Parents Taking Care of Themselves

GOAL: For parents to see their own well-being as necessary to the well-being of their children and to develop personal strategies for self-care

Healthy Parents, Healthy Children

The ultimate source of a child's emotional stability is a parent's emotional stability. *The stability of parents has proven to be associated with the stability of children.* Studies tell us that children have a good chance of successfully coping with a parental breakup if they have at least one well-adjusted, stable parent. Fortunately, each parent has control of at least one. Parents should appreciate that their personal well-being is not a luxury. It is, for sure, one of the most important things they can do to help their children through the challenges of their breakup. Make no mistake: For parents to take care of themselves is to take care of their children!

— Checklist —
Why Parental Self-Care Is So Important

Diminished Quality of Parenting

Being in the presence of an upset parent is stressful. Normally, children would turn to a parent for comfort when they are upset by a disturbing event, such as a child looking to be held during a thunderstorm. But what does a child do when the thunderstorm is coming from an intensely upset parent, perhaps the child's only source of comfort? It is well documented that chronic high stress impairs the quality of parenting. It's human nature. *When upset, parents become less attentive, less engaged, and intolerant.* In their parenting, they become more easily annoyed, quick tempered, and punitive with the children.

Eclipsed Emotional Availability

Even when parents are physically present with their children, they may find their minds to be elsewhere racing with upsetting thoughts and emotions. Intrusive thoughts can flood the mind, keeping parents in a constant state of anxiety, worry, or anger. Such mental distractions can cause parents to miss precious moments or even the critical needs of their children. *The love and attentive focus that parents would normally have for their children can be eclipsed by their racing minds.*

Parents Unaware of Their Own Pain

It is useful for parents to be aware of their own stress levels. As mentioned, it can impair parenting. Also, stressed-out parents are likely to be highly reactive to interparent conflict which, in turn, will keep them anxious and overwhelmed. What if emotional pain could be seen as a physical injury, such as a bruise, burn, or black-and-blue mark? Parents might ask themselves just how bruised, burned, or black and blue they might be? *Awareness of their own pain is a good first step toward parental self-care.*

Children Thrive with Parental Warmth

All children need the attention and love of their parents. Children going through a family breakup will need that parental nurturing more than ever. The challenges of a breakup naturally diminish the time and energy resources of parents. *Parents who are able to adequately care for themselves will have the emotional availability that children need from them.* Giving the warmth children need will refresh parental well-being as well.

— Worksheet —

Parents Taking Care of Themselves

Ideas and Strategies for Parental Self-Care

Parents Focusing on Their Own Well-Being

Despite the emotional pain that often comes with a breakup, children need their parents to be physically and emotionally healthy. Parents in extreme distress should commit to improving their health and well-being.

Notes: _____

Acceptance

Acceptance does not suggest an approval of unwanted family changes. It is simply an accommodation to the truth, even if it is a painful truth. Ultimately, acceptance is the foundation for positive changes, personal development, and one day, maybe even gratitude.

Notes: _____

Not an End, but a New Beginning

A breakup can overwhelm parents with a profound sense of grief: It's over! The end! When the veil of grief begins to lift, parents will see that, at the very end of the ending, there will be a passageway to a new beginning. Heal and it will appear.

Notes: _____

Take It One Day at a Time

One of the best ways to get through difficult times is to focus on just having one good day at a time. No big life changes. Just a simple desire to have one good day: today. Just by sweetening a day with small comforts and taking a small step in the right direction can turn any day into a good day. Surely, it can be done at least once. Do it today. Then, do it again tomorrow.

Notes: _____

Live Well to Feel Well

Parents should make a commitment to have their lives defined by healthy intentions rather than unwanted circumstances. Parents should prepare and follow a list of good intentions: Today, I will help someone, be kind, play with the children, exercise, enjoy a meal, call a friend, read something inspiring, express gratitude. Live well to feel well.

Notes: _____

Stay Present in the Moment

Parents should be mindful to not let upsetting thoughts and feelings distract them from being fully present when they are with their children. To counter the effects of intrusive thoughts, parents should use their senses to hyper-focus on the children. Saturate the senses with the children: get close, make eye contact, really listen, touch, feel, engage, hug, play, laugh. The mind will quiet.

Notes: _____

Live with Gratitude

Despite the pain of going through a breakup, parents should take time to remind themselves of the small and large reasons they have to remain grateful. Writing daily in a gratitude journal will balance a stressful mind with peaceful thoughts.

Notes: _____

Exercise Regularly

Exercise is well known to remove tension from the body and soothe the mind. Parents should identify the types of workouts they most enjoy and best fit their schedule. Combining exercise with nature, people, music, or pets will enhance the experience.

Notes: _____

Balance Stress with Relaxation

Most parents will already have a few healthy ways to relax. They should practice them routinely. Consider new ways to find peace and calm: listening to music, nature walks, meditation, yoga, journaling, inspirational or spiritual readings.

Notes: _____

Build a Support Group

Parents should establish an inner circle of people who support them. Perhaps see a therapist. Stay close to these people, share your feelings. Avoid posting interparent conflict details on social media, as it tends to inflame conflict and perpetuate distress.

Notes: _____

Disengaging from Parent Conflict

GOAL: For parents to be empowered with strategies to disengage
from conflict and engage in healthy co-parenting

Conflict between parents is one of the most significant reasons children are hurt by parental breakups. That is because interparent conflict is stressful and it interferes with effective co-parenting. For example, conflict can intensify disputes over custody, new partners, and relocation. Even smaller issues, like bedtime and homework routines, get elevated into larger disputes. Some degree of interparent conflict is to be expected for separating couples; most families adjust with time. However, high-conflict parents with long histories of relationship and family instability will jeopardize the well-being of their children for years to come. Separation will not necessarily put an end to conflict for these parents. For them, separation often adds more stress to their conflict. Therefore, management of conflict between parents and among other family members is critical to protecting and promoting the well-being of children. It is an essential part of a healthy outcome.

Children Need Parents to Bring Out Their Best Side

Just When Children Need a Parent's Best Side

For many years following a breakup, children will need their parents to provide their best efforts at shielding them from the harmful effects of being caught in the middle of their conflict. At the same time, they will need their parents to craft healthy two-home families where children can thrive, be loved, and be supported by both parents. This will require both parents to be at their best.

Conflict Brings Out a Parent's Worst Side

Just when children need their parents to be at their best, interparent conflict often brings out their very worst. Conflict has the potential to keep parents in a constant state of alarm, each anticipating some form of trouble or drama from the other. The needs of children can be eclipsed as parents become hyper-focused on each other.

Parenting Poisoned by Partner Problems

A former couple with serious, unresolved relationship problems will find it difficult, and maybe even impossible, to stay focused on their children. Attempts at parenting can quickly turn into opportunities for airing grievances, venting feelings, or criticizing each other. *Parenting becomes a mask for continued relationship fighting.* This is a toxic situation for children.

Appreciate that Both Needs Exist

It is important for conflicted parents to recognize their competing desires. As former couples, they may have *unresolved issues and painful feelings that keep them at odds with one another.* They might have a need to argue or completely avoid each other. The mere presence of the other parent may trigger irrepressible conflict reactions. At the same time, there is a *competing need to care for the children. Both exist!*

Quiet the Worst and Bring Out the Best

Being aware of their inner competing motives will help parents recognize their adversarial impulses and override them with a shared desire to care for their children. In each parenting moment, parents should remind themselves that *their children need them to steady themselves and remain child centered.*

A Subgroup of Highly Conflicted Parents

Separating parents can be classified as being mildly, moderately, or highly conflicted. Risk for children having adjustment problems is most associated with highly conflicted parents, estimated to be as high as 25 percent of all separating parents. *They are a subgroup with interparent conflict that is likely to be intense, long lasting, and difficult to resolve.* High-conflict parents can be driven by unresolvable disputes, with both parents seeing themselves as right and the other as wrong. Some high conflict is driven by one or both parents who are fragile or unstable as a result of serious psychiatric disorders, addiction, criminality, or violence. High-conflict parents are often unable to manage their conflict or shield their children from it without effective interventions. For these parents, counseling alone is not likely to be effective. Nor is litigation alone likely to be effective. The best intervention is likely to be a combination of legal and mental health services. See the section on "Managing Safety Issues."

— Worksheet —
Dynamics of High Conflict

Interparent conflict is an expression of a relationship between two parents. Each parent brings their individual personalities and unique coping styles to their co-parenting relationship. Each parent brings biases and perceptual filters that will influence how they see each other. Each parent brings a personal pattern of acting and reacting to the other parent. Understanding characteristics of interparent conflict will offer insights that can help parents disengage from conflict. If conflict is a product of the interaction of two people, then conflict can change when one person changes.

PLEASE NOTE: The following description of the elements of interparent conflict should not be taken to suggest that there is some generalized, one-size-fits-all, description of interparent conflict. The presentation of basic elements of conflict is meant to provide parents with specific insights on how conflict works for the purpose of developing strategies on how they might diminish or disengage from it.

Poorly Adjusted Parents Prone to Conflict

For many parents, breakups are experienced as personal life crises. Even well-adjusted parents will find an upper limit on how much stress they can tolerate before becoming overwhelmed and highly reactive in a conflict relationship. Poorly adjusted parents will be even more intensely reactive to conflict. Among high-conflict parents, there will also be individuals with serious adjustment problems, such as mental health, addiction, anger, criminality, or control issues. Thus, a core characteristic of interparent conflict occurs when one or both parents have adjustment problems that diminishes their self-control and makes them more impulsive or avoidant. One poorly adjusted parent can impair a co-parenting relationship. Two poorly adjusted parents can make it toxic. Where there are safety concerns, parents should read the section on "Managing Safety Issues." Using this insight, how can parents change themselves so they might diminish or disengage from interparent conflict?

Notes: _____

Poor Personal Coping Skills

Poorly adjusted parents are likely to feel more unstable and threatened by the strains of a conflicted interparent relationship. Feeling overwhelmed, these parents often cope in unhealthy ways. Criticizing and demeaning the other parent is a common problem-solving strategy. Venting and exploding on the other parent relieves a parent of stress in the moment but further aggravates a conflicted interparent relationship. A parent refusing to speak to the other parent solves a personal avoidance need but adds to conflict in the parenting relationship. Attempts to co-parent can quickly escalate into intolerable arguments with parents making points about each other rather than solving problems for the children. Repeated efforts to solve problems with ineffective coping skills will cause continued frustration and increase long-term instability. Using this insight, how can parents change themselves so they might diminish or disengage from interparent conflict?

Notes: _____

Fixed Images of Each Other

Conflicted relationship interactions before, during, and after separation contribute to forging negative perceptions parents have of each other. Each is certain they know the "true" picture of the other. They come to grand conclusions about each other. Fixed perceptual pictures form and are used to explain everything about the breakup and subsequent conflict. Situational facts are cherry-picked to match convenient truths held by either parent. Facts to the contrary are dismissed as manipulations. In different ways, both parents allege they have been victimized by the other parent. Both feel provoked and compelled to defend themselves. *These perceptions can liberate parents from treating each other with respect, fairness, or civility.* Harsh judgments can be made to terminate the rights of a parent, say things that alienate the children, or even manipulate the legal system. The ends now justify the means. Using this insight, how can parents change themselves so they might diminish or disengage from interparent conflict?

Notes: _____

Blaming the Other Parent

With their fixed images of each other intact, high-conflict parents set out to convince each other of their bad intentions, poor character, and threatening motives. In streams of gotcha moments, they will point out proof of the other's badness. Unable to convince bad actors of their badness, offended parents respond with their own reactions—then seen as offensive by the other. More gotcha moments are claimed and argued about in text-messaging wars. Neither parent can believe the other parent does not get it. Since they believe the problem lies in the other parent, neither parent has the power to solve co-parenting problems. Accusations continue with greater volume. The mutual demand of "my way" or "no way" puts the co-parenting relationship in a state of paralysis. Using this insight, how can parents change themselves so they might diminish or disengage from interparent conflict?

Notes: _____

Conflicting Roles of Ex-partner and Co-parent

Separating parents have two relationships: They are soon to be ex-partners and continue to be parents. These two roles are going in opposite directions. A breakup sends ex-partners in separate directions. As parents, they recognize a need to come together for the children. At the same time, one or both may have a strong need to get away from the other. These ex-partner and co-parent roles are at cross purposes. Unwanted partners easily turn into unwelcomed co-parents. Emotionally, each parent is both an "injured partner" and a "caring parent." It will take a well-adjusted parent to separate those two roles. Poorly adjusted parents with poor coping skills will find it nearly impossible to engage in co-operative co-parenting. High-conflict parents will have co-parenting discussions that are essentially unresolved arguments between two injured partners. Using this insight, how can parents change themselves so they might diminish or disengage from interparent conflict?

Notes: _____

Pursuit of Social Justice

Two parents, each insisting they have been injured by the other, may *seek some form of social justice where they would be entitled to have the other parent admit, apologize, compensate, or maybe even be punished* for their injurious deeds. But neither is willing to submit to the blame-based solutions demanded by the other parent. They eventually stop trying to convince each other and turn to convincing others—family, friends, sometimes their children, and eventually a judge with whom they believe they will finally find "justice." Sometimes, they are disappointed in the outcome. Using this insight, how can parents change themselves so they might diminish or disengage from interparent conflict?

Notes: _____

Same Parents: Two Problem-Solving Discussions

Two versions of the same parents trying to address their child's school problem

Two Injured Partners
Proving Points About Each Other

Parent A: "So, what do you want to do?"

Parent B: "I am helping our son with homework all the time. I think it's time for you to step up."

Parent A: "That's not true. I work with him all the time. He tells me that you don't help him at all, and when he does ask you for help, you get mad at him."

Parent B: "My mother is a retired teacher and she tells me I am doing the right thing."

Parent A: "Don't get me started on your mother. She was the worst teacher ever!"

Parent B: "You never cared about your own schooling. Why would you care about our son's schooling?"

Parent A: Hangs up. No solution.

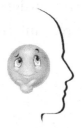 

Two Caring Parents
Solving the Problem

Parent A: "So, what do you want to do?"

Parent B: "I think we should get a better idea of our son's reading problem."

Parent A: "Maybe we could ask for an evaluation by the school's reading specialist."

Parent B: "Ok, let's do that. I also think we should both emphasize the importance of reading to our son."

Parent A: "I agree. Let's each commit to making reading a homework priority when he is staying with us."

Parent B: "Ok. Why don't we try to have him read for 30 minutes by himself and then we would have him tell us about what he has read."

Parent A: "Sounds good."

The Parenting Challenge: Do I want to . . .

Parents are empowered when they become aware of their inner conflicted motives and how they have the potential to contaminate parenting discussions. The injured partner within them will create anxiety and keep them on high alert searching for problems in the other parent. Just thinking about the other parent can cause them to spiral more deeply into conflict. At the same time, there resides within each of them a caring parent who is aware of their reactive tendencies and how those impulses can interfere with parenting. *With this awareness, they can resist and override the impulse to prove points about each other.* They will then be empowered to redirect their efforts into solving problems for the children. Each parent should take personal responsibility to remain mindful of their mixed motives and stay centered as a caring parent.

— Worksheet —

Disengage from Parenting as Injured Partners

Start with Court-ordered Time Sharing

A highly detailed Court order, called a Parenting Plan, can provide needed structure. It should define with specificity time sharing, holidays, vacations, exchanges, driving responsibilities, and interparent communications.

Notes: _____

Maintain Appropriate Boundaries

High-conflict parents should set boundaries to limit their unproductive talk and time together. They should consider time-sharing schedules to reduce the number of exchanges, consider neutral exchanges where children are picked up and dropped off at school, and use a therapist, mediator, or co-parenting coordinator to host parenting talks.

Notes: _____

Pursue a Strategy of Disengagement

Think of conflict as the sound of two hands clapping. It takes two hands to make that sound. What if one hand quit? What is the sound of one hand clapping? Conflict is a relationship dynamic. It takes two parents to make the sound of conflict. From this perspective, if one person changes, the relationship changes. *Conflict can be reduced or stopped when just one parent disengages from it.*

Notes: _____

Break the Action-Reaction Pattern of Conflict

Newton's Cradle is another useful metaphor in understanding how conflict might be stopped. Like the steel balls, conflict functions with parents engaged in a pattern of actions and reactions. How do you get the steel balls to stop clicking? By withholding a reaction on either side. *When parents stop reacting, the action-reaction pattern will begin to break down.*

Notes: _____

Don't Provoke

Parents who engage the other parent with criticism, insults, blame, or name calling will very predictably trigger a defensive or adversarial response in the other parent. Parents should recognize when they are acting as an injured partner and avoid provoking the other parent. Doing so will begin to break down the action-reaction conflict pattern.

Notes: _____

Don't React to Provocation

High-conflict parents who are mindful of their mixed motives can restrain themselves and avoid reacting in ways that perpetuate the action-reaction cycle of conflict. This too will help to break down the action-reaction pattern of conflict.

Notes: _____

— *Worksheet* —

Engage as Caring Parents

Get Centered as a Mom or Dad

Parents should take individual responsibility to bring themselves to co-parenting discussions grounded in an internal emotional state of being a caring parent. When starting a discussion, they should consider sharing pictures of the children, reflecting on proud parental moments, and share pleasant memories of the children, all meant to evoke child-centeredness in self and the other parent.

Notes: _____

Pursue Dedicated Co-parenting Discussions

Parents should approach the co-parenting discussions fully disciplined to have conversations that are dedicated exclusively to the children. Parents should seek to activate an action-reaction pattern of child-centered co-parenting. They should each take responsibility to get "back on task of parenting" should they slip into conflict interactions.

Notes: _____

Pursue a Vision of a Healthy Two-Home Family

With an awareness that there are many children who are thriving in healthy two-home families, parents should take a solution-focused approach to developing their own version of a healthy two-home family. Start by imagining a solution where children are safe and well-cared for, where parents avoid conflict and move on in their own lives. *There is a best-case scenario for every family*. Parents are unlikely to find it unless they are looking for it. Imagine it and then take steps to make it come true.

Notes: _____

Realize Parental Shared Interests

While parents may have their differences, they do have shared interests: Both want their children to be healthy, safe, well-adjusted, good students, and have healthy relationships. Parents can pursue these values jointly or separately.

Notes: _____

Give Children at Least One Conflict-Free Home

Studies suggest that the well-being of children can be protected if at least one parent gives them a conflict-free home. *Each parent has power to give children needed family stability* by providing one healthy home environment.

Notes: _____

Consider the Other Parent's Love of Children

Conflicted parents often see the other parent through a lens of distrust, shaped by past partner issues. Parents should consider taking a chance on the other parent's love for their children. *This new lens may open a door to hope.*

Notes: _____

Seeing Problems Through the Eyes of a Child

GOAL: For parents to see the emotional needs of their children as being different from their own

The Little Chair Exercise

Parental cooperation can be compromised when unresolved "partner" problems get conflated or mixed into "parent" discussions. This often leads to parents having partner arguments that will hamstring their ability to work together. *This Little Chair Exercise will help parents reverse this conflation by separating the parent issues from partner issues.* There will always be at least three possible viewpoints or truths that are involved in any childcare decision: those of mom, dad, and the children. This exercise will help parents to see the needs of their children more clearly. To conduct this exercise, parents will first need to identify the topic or problem. In the case study presented below, one parent had their six-year-old son evaluated for ADHD. The boy was diagnosed with ADHD. That parent started the child on ADHD medication. At the point of this intervention, one parent was medicating the child and the other refused to do so. The child attended school three days a week having taken medication and two days without medication.

Mom had a point of view. She was sure that she was right, and dad was wrong. Dad had a different point of view. He was sure that he was right, and mom was wrong. They were ultimately able to put their views and demands aside to "sit in the little chair" and view the problem from their son's point of view. This helped them to find an agreeable solution.

Three Points of View

Parent A's Perspective

Parent A was worried that their six-year-old son was having difficulty staying focused in class. Parents were getting reports from school that their son was impulsive and was distracting other students in class. Parent A had the child evaluated and started ADHD medication. Parent A dismissed Parent B's disagreement as something that Parent B always does. Consequently, Parent A concluded that there is no point in seeking a consensus.

Parent B's Perspective

Parent B was not told that Parent A was seeking an evaluation for ADHD. This parent vehemently disagreed with their child taking ADHD medication and refused to administer the medication. Parent B did not believe the child had ADHD. Instead, this parent believed the child's behavior was a product of Parent A abruptly moving out of the home and moving in with a new partner who had several young children.

Little Chair View of Child's Perspective

Both parents were led by a therapist to see the problem from their son's point of view, symbolized by the little chair. Their son was likely to be confused by being medicated for some days and not others. He would have been confused by being told he did and did not have ADHD. He would have been confused by abruptly moving into a new stepfamily arrangement. His parents were able to appreciate that he might potentially have both problems. They were able to understand that their parental dispute resulting in the child attending school with and without medication each week was not a healthy outcome.

Little Chair Solution

The parents agreed to stop medication and had the child work with an ADHD specialist to learn adaptive skills, as well as seeking family therapy to help the child adjust to the family changes. They further agreed to work this plan for three months and, if no progress was seen, they would reconsider the ADHD medication.

Keeping Children Out of the Middle

*GOAL: For parents to see how their own interparent conflict actions
and reactions may have negative effects on the children*

Children of separating and divorcing parents can be expected to be highly sensitive to the conflicted feelings that exist between their parents. The intensity of parental feelings and the proximity of children makes it very challenging to keep children out of the middle. However, *with mindful intentions, parents can effectively protect their children* from one of the most significant factors that puts children at risk for emotional and behavioral problems: direct exposure to parental conflict. Children will benefit even if only one parent were to shield them from parental conflict.

— Worksheet —

How to Keep Children Out of the Middle

AVOID: Making Children Feel Like They Have to Take Sides

Parents should assume that children need and want the love of both parents. Parents who expose children to their negative feelings toward the other parent will commonly see their children align or keep silent when they criticize the other parent. *When children are aligning with one parent, they are committing an act of disloyalty to the other parent.* They may become double agents as they try to please both parents.

Notes: _____

AVOID: Arguing in Front of the Children

Avoid allowing children to directly witness parental conflict: arguing at exchanges, children overhearing parental phone arguments, or overhearing parental criticisms to other people in person or by phone.

Notes: _____

AVOID: Asking Children to Keep Secrets

Avoid asking children to keep large adult secrets: where they live, with whom they live, or long-distance travel plans. Avoid little secrets, too: diet, activities participation, or school attendance. Parents should work out their boundary issues and give children permission to share appropriate information.

Notes: _____

AVOID: Quizzing the Children About the Other Parent

Avoid asking children intrusive questions about the other parent. Children are put in the middle when parents use them as the informational source in making allegations against the other parent.

Notes: _____

AVOID: Asking the Children to Carry Painful Messages

Children should not be asked to call the other parent to extend time, say that they will not be returned on time, or seek permission to do something on the other parent's time. These are adult responsibilities.

Notes: _____

AVOID: Sending Children Back and Forth Asking for Money

Parents may disagree over who should cover specific expenses for the children. They should work it out together or seek a litigated decision. Children should not be sent back and forth asking for money.

Notes: _____

AVOID: Saying Mean Things About the Other Parent

Many children suffer when one or both parents go on unfiltered critical rants about the other parent. This can make children insecure, anxious, take sides, or become overly avoidant of conflict.

Notes: _____

AVOID: Making Children Feel Responsible for Adult Decisions

Anxious children will be inclined to say yes to parental requests: Would you prefer to live with me? Do you mind if I have my new partner join us? Want to do a fun thing on the other parent's time?

Notes: _____

Empowering Children to Protect Themselves

Parents will not always be able to protect children from exposure to their conflict. However, children can be taught to protect themselves from conflict. Parents can do this by giving children permission to tell their parents or others when something is said or done that is hurtful or disturbing to them. *Teach them respectful ways to take themselves out of the middle of conflict.* Parents should try giving their children a way to notify them should they slip and say or do something that upsets the children.

Examples of Children Empowered to Respectfully Take Themselves Out of the Middle

— Worksheet —

Promise Children Not to Put Them in the Middle

Parental breakups are painful for children. Decades of research, as well as common sense, tells us not to put the children in the middle of parental conflict. Even with good intentions, it is easier said than done. Parents should consider using the Kids First Promise presented below. First, parents should review the promises with their children and commit to not putting them in the middle. Parents should sign the form and give children permission to remind them if they should slip and break a promise.

Kids First Promise
Protect Children from Parent Conflict
Promise from Mom or Dad:

I promise NOT to . . .
*Make you take sides
*Argue in front of you
*Ask you to keep secrets
*Quiz you about your other parent
*Make you my messenger
*Send you back and forth asking for money
*Say mean things to you about your mom or dad

_____

Signature of Parent(s)

Managing Safety Issues

*GOAL: For parents to be aware of community and legal services
that are often Court-ordered to address safety issues*

— Worksheet —

Court-Ordered Interventions

Court Support

When the behavior of one or both parents potentially jeopardizes the welfare of children, the Court may order interventions designed to keep children safe. *The interventions usually address serious problems such as addiction, serious mental illness, violence, neglect, or abuse.* Parents who fail to comply with Court-ordered interventions could be held in contempt of Court and be subject to fines or imprisonment. The Court may require compliance with an order as condition for visitation with the children. The interventions listed below may not be available in all jurisdictions. Interventions will vary in the degree of intrusiveness to the family. Parents should consult their attorneys in petitioning the Court for an intervention. Responsibility for costs should be addressed in the petition and order.

Notes: _____

Stay Focused on Safety

Allegations asserting that a parent represents a danger to the other parent or children may result in an outcome that limits parental access to the chil-

---

55

dren. Courts might be inclined, at least initially, to err on the side of safety. Parental conflict often intensifies as parents fight over who is the real problem. *Sometimes it is best to shift the focus away from who is the problem and move toward finding a solution that is agreeable to everyone: safety.* No one should be against safety. For example, if the safety issue is alleged drug abuse, safety can be defined as sobriety. Being drug free can be independently monitored by a neutral third party. Avoiding long, protracted arguments about injustice and, instead, focusing on meeting the defined conditions of safety can open the door to a parent's resumed access to the children.

Notes: _____

Child Protective Services

Each state has child protective services that will investigate reports of possible child abuse, provide protection for children from being abused, as well as rehabilitation services for children and parents. Professionals in education, law, mental health, healthcare, and other fields are mandated reporters who are required to make reports of suspected child abuse. For further information, search "How to make a report of child abuse."

Notes: _____

Domestic Violence

Different Rules for Domestic Violence

Under the genuine threat of domestic violence, vulnerable parents should avoid "working with" dangerous partners, as doing so might put them in harm's way. In effect, there is a different set of rules where the real threat of violence exists. Of greatest concern, are those individuals who seek to dominate and control others with intimidation and violence.

Notes: _____

Cooperation May Be Possible for Some

Researchers have reported that domestic violence might be categorized into different types or profiles. For example, someone without a violent history might have become intimidating on only one occasion. This aggression might be seen as a result of the frustration and conflict in the couple/parenting relationship. This profile stands in contrast to a controlling batterer with a long history of violent behavior and substance addiction. Thus, we might consider that some individuals who acted aggressively might have the potential to co-parent with appropriate precautions and interventions. Knowing this, some parents may cautiously consider some measure of co-parenting, such as limited communication to discuss parenting issues or they might consider meeting jointly with a therapist or mediator. *Vulnerable parents dealing with violent, controlling types are advised to avoid this alternative.*

Protection Orders

Individuals who have been victims of violent acts or who are in fear of their safety may seek protection or restraining orders from the Court. There are Court orders that provide strict limits on the behavior of aggressive individuals. These Court orders might restrict them from being in the same location and prohibit them from any form of communication with the victim. Protection orders can include the children if the behavior of the offending parent endangers the children.

Generally, temporary orders are issued and are reviewed at subsequent Court hearings where defendants are given an opportunity to present a defense against the accusation. Final agreements or judicial decisions are likely to be made at that time. Weapons are usually confiscated with protection orders. It is also common for orders to include interventions such as treatment for substance abuse, anger management, or mental health counseling. Some orders may allow limited parent communication or for the parents to be together for co-parenting counseling. Monitoring compliance with protection orders is essentially up to the victim since police cannot provide around-the-clock personal protection. Individuals reported to have violated their protection orders are subject to arrest and incarceration. It is an unfortunate fact that protection orders are occasionally misused and abused. For example, there are some who obtain orders only to ignore or drop them when they reconcile with their partners. Worse, there are others who seek protection orders by making false allegations to gain an advantage in child custody litigation. Such abuse weakens this vital intervention.

Notes: _____

— Checklist —

Other Interventions Subject to Court Order

Interventions: By Agreement or Court Order

Interventions presented in this list are meant to advance and protect the well-being of children. Parents might agree to pursue an intervention on their own without a written agreement or a Court order. Parents who agree on an intervention can also agree to have it submitted to the Court and made into an order. The Court may impose interventions if it serves the best interests of the children. Parents should consult with their attorneys for guidance on how to pursue Court-ordered interventions.

Intervention: Drug and Alcohol Evaluations and Treatment

Through agreement or Court order, one or both parents might be ordered to receive a drug and alcohol evaluation. They would also likely be ordered to follow any treatment recommendations listed in the evaluation report, possibly including periodic drug testing.

Intervention: Anger Management Evaluations and Treatment

When parental volatility raises concern about safety to the other parent or children, the Court can be petitioned to order an anger management evaluation. They might also be required to seek individual anger management therapy or to take an anger management class.

Intervention: Mental Health Evaluations and Treatment

When parental conduct appears to be impaired by possible serious psychiatric conditions, the Court might be petitioned to order a psychiatric evaluation of one or both parents. Evaluations might be conducted by mental health professionals in private practice or in a social service agency.

Intervention: Co-parenting Counseling or Coordination

Some parents might privately pursue co-parenting counseling as they make the transition into two-home households. The Family Court Administrator's Office would be a good source to find an experienced therapist. *Highly conflicted parents might agree, or the Court might order them into co-parenting counseling or co-parenting coordination.* Co-parenting co-ordinators may be given authority to arbitrate decisions of conflicted parents. Co-parenting counselors or coordinators may be given permission or ordered to provide reports to the Court.

Intervention: Reunification Therapy

Following a parental breakup, some children will refuse to spend time with one of their parents. A mental health professional can be appointed to help reunify a parent with an estranged child. Parents should be careful to select a professional trained and experienced in facilitating parent-child reunification. *That professional should use a family systems approach* that includes the preferred parent as well as the rejected parent in the reunification effort.

Intervention: Guardian Ad Litem

A Guardian Ad Litem generally is an attorney appointed by the Court to either represent the best interests of the children or serve as an attorney for the children. A guardian will meet with children, as well as parents. Guardians will make reports and recommendations to the Court.

Intervention: Child Custody Evaluations

Sometimes parents are unable to come to an agreement on how they will share time with the children. Parents may stipulate to a child custody evaluation or the Court might order one. In the evaluation, a mental health professional will be appointed to assess each parent, the children, and parent-child relationships as a basis for making recommendations to the Court for custody schedules.

Intervention: Supervised Visitation

When there is a suspicion that the children might not be safe in the care of a parent, the Court might order supervised visitation. In this intervention, a parent will be allowed to spend time with the children in the presence of a third party who serves as the supervisor. Potential supervisors might include the other parent, a family member, a social service agency, or a paid supervisor who will accompany the parent and child in the community.

Intervention: Parent Divorce Education

Many Family Courts order parents who have filed for custody or divorce to take a parent divorce education program. Typically, they are about four hours long. These programs are designed to sensitize parents to attend to the needs of the children as they make the transition into two-home families.

Intervention: Parent Skills Training

Adolescent parents or other new parents may benefit from participating in classes for new parents or meet with healthcare professionals to ensure they are adequately attending to the needs of children.

Intervention: Parenting Skills for Children with Special Needs

Children who have special needs may need specialized care from their parents. This might include children who have chronic health conditions, emotional or behavioral problems, conditions that might impair learning, or conditions that may interfere with their ability to cope with their lives at home or in the community. Parents might meet with selected professionals or participate in selective classes.

Intervention: Therapy for Children

Research suggests that children will benefit from having some supportive counseling as they adjust to the breakup of their parents. Once separated, legal custody is assigned to one or both parents. Usually, legal custody is shared by both parents. Consequently, both parents will need to consent to the therapy. In the absence of that consent, parents can seek a Court order for the therapy.

Intervention: Family Therapy

In family therapy, a family is viewed as a system with many parts and multiple interactive relationships. When a family system is dysfunctional, it tends to put a lot of pressure on individual parts of the family, especially children when there is interparent conflict. This intervention focuses on bringing relief to children by altering parental and child-parent relationships.

Telling the Children

GOAL: For parents to explain to children how their lives will be changing in a child centered and reassuring manner

Children need some idea of what their lives might look like after the breakup. *They need more than an announcement that life as they knew it is over. That alone will leave them anxious and insecure.* While the specific details may not be knowable at the time of the announcement, parents can share their intentions of what they are hoping for in the future. Parents should plan and deliver a reassuring message that will leave the children feeling safe and secure in their family relationships. *If the breakup has already occurred, children will still need a reassuring message about the future.* Example: "I'm not sure where we will find a house, but it will be in the same school district."

Girl Tells Story of a Child-Centered Explanation

"I remember that day like it was yesterday. I was six years old. One day my parents asked me to come into the living room and sit down. Somehow, I knew what they were about to tell me. They said, 'You know your mommy loves you and your daddy loves you, but we don't love each other like a husband and wife should.' They told me that they were going to separate. Then they reminded me that we would still be a family. We would just be living in two homes. They told me that all the family members I love would still be in my life. I was crying and they were crying. I went to my room and cried some more. They each came to me one at a time to comfort me. They told me we could talk about it more tomorrow and that I could ask any questions that I wanted. Looking back, they made it so easy for me."

Melissa, 19 years old

Age 6 when parents separated

What Melissa's Parents Did Well

- Reassurance: Melissa was reminded that she still had a family that included all the people she loved
- Child-centered: Parents described family changes from Melissa's point of view
- Nurturing: In words and actions, both parents focused on soothing their daughter
- Adult boundary: There was no blame directed at either parent
- Questions: Melissa was encouraged to ask questions the next day
- Memory: The event of being told will never be forgotten. This child's memory was a loving one

Example of an Adult High-Conflict Version of a Breakup

Two parents were in marriage counseling. One was having an affair and the other did not know about it. The parent having the affair finally disclosed the affair and announced the intention to separate and get divorced. The parent being left was hurt and angry. The parent being left said, "I want you out of the house today and I am going to tell our son what you have done!" This child was about to be told an adult-centered version of the breakup. He would likely have remained stuck in the middle, as the other parent would likely offer another version of this adult story.

How These Parents Corrected Themselves

Both parents cared deeply about their child. They were ultimately able to see that using their raw pain as a message to announce the breakup could be hurtful to their son. After concluding that it was best to separate, they turned their attention to how it could best be done for their son. They decided to stay together for the next four weeks and use that time to prepare themselves and their son for the separation. They ultimately told the boy together. Their son had adequate time to adjust to the message while his parents were still together. They even visited the departing parent's new apartment together. Both parents were surprised at how well their son adjusted to the breakup.

Resetting Parenting Boundaries

GOAL: For parents to assess and develop a new set of boundaries that will provide children with two healthy home environments

A Need to Revise Boundaries

Parental breakups will significantly alter the functional boundaries of family life. Parents should expect to find that their old boundaries will no longer work once they are separated. As ex-partners, high-conflict parents may have a powerful need for a terminal boundary with the other parent, one that has no access or communication. At the same time, there is a need for co-parents to have boundaries that allow for information sharing and communication. Imposing an oversized ex-partner boundary may impair parenting functions. *Parents should seek to redefine boundaries that respect the individual needs of both parents while providing an appropriate medium for co-parenting.*

Too Restrictive, Too Porous

If boundaries are effective, they will allow for healthy interactions and limit unhealthy functions. When they are ineffective, they seem to do just the opposite, allowing conflict to contaminate both individual and shared parenting. At one end of dysfunction, needed boundaries are either nonexistent or too porous. When this happens, children might be exposed to safety risks, conflict, unwanted intrusions, and parental interference. At the other end of dysfunction, boundaries can be too large, restrictive, and rigid. When this happens, a parent may be blocked from seeing, communicating, or getting information about the children. *Boundaries can be too small or too large.*

— Worksheet —

Interparent Boundary Options

 Open Boundary: Good for Highly Cooperative Parenting

This minimal boundary allows for significant overlap between the lives of parents. It is ideal for low conflict, highly cooperative parents. Such parents communicate well, might have shared birthday parties, attend child events together, and even visit each other's home. This degree of overlap is not recommended for highly conflicted parents, as it is likely to create stress for children.

Notes: _____

 Moderate Boundary: Coordinated Parenting

This boundary allows for just enough overlap to manage co-parent responsibilities while maintaining limited access into each other's life. These parents communicate well enough and are civil toward each other, especially in front of the children. This arrangement may be good for low to moderately conflicted parents but might still be challenging for highly conflicted parents.

Notes: _____

 Closed Boundary: Separate and Parallel Parenting

In this parallel structure, parental interaction is avoided or kept to a minimum. Both parents independently contribute to the care of the children. This strict boundary limits interaction between high-conflict parents. Under this arrangement, children might be exchanged at a neutral place, such as school, with parents having no contact with each other. Their parenting efforts might be coordinated by a Court-appointed professional.

Notes: _____

— Worksheet —

Review of Critical Interparent Boundaries

Honor Residential and Privacy Boundaries

Both parents should honor a boundary that allows each to enjoy their homes and personal life space free of worry about unwanted intrusions by the other parent.

Notes: _____

Respect Boundary of the Other Parent's Time with the Children

Parents should avoid discussing or making plans with the children that fall on the other parent's scheduled time with the children without first getting approval from that parent. Getting the children excited about doing something on the other parent's time without consent might be seen as manipulative.

Notes: _____

Avoid Interfering with the Other Parent's Authority

Parents probably have different parenting styles. Children must get used to being supervised by two separate authority figures. Criticizing the other parent's authority violates a boundary with the other parent's authority over the children. It will give children permission to be defiant with that parent.

Notes: _____

Establish Boundaries for Parent-Child Communications

Children should be allowed privacy while speaking by phone with the out-of-custody parent. Avoid putting phone calls on speakerphone or tacking on adult business at the end of the parent-child calls.

Notes: _____

Set Boundaries for New Partners

Biological parents should assume the primary role of providing expectations and discipline to the children. Children living in stepfamilies will value some one-on-one time with their biological parents.

Notes: _____

Maintain Appropriate Adult Boundaries

Avoid elevating children to adult roles by turning to them for advice on dating, leaning on them for emotional support, seeking custody alliances, or sharing other inappropriate adult information.

Notes: _____

Shield Children from Parental Conflict

Parents should avoid having their children witness interparent conflict at the exchanges, when they communicate, showing text messages, or overhearing one parent criticizing the other parent.

Notes: _____

Avoid Saturating Children in Parental Grief

Parents should avoid overexposing their children to deep levels of emotional pain, anxiety, grief, or anger. Children who are enmeshed with a suffering parent will feel many of the same emotions.

Notes: _____

Co-parenting Communication

GOAL: For parents to set aside their personal reactions and effectively share information, make decisions, and solve problems for the children

The Communication Challenge

Imagine that you were a patient in the hospital who was totally dependent on the care of a group of doctors, nurses, and staff members who did not speak to each other. Or worse, every time they tried to discuss your treatment, they got into a huge fight and stormed out of the room. You would have to imagine that your well-being might be at risk. So, it is with children of separated parents who are unable to communicate with each other. The communication challenge: *Parents must find ways to share childcare information, make child-centered co-parenting decisions, keep unresolved partner issues out of parent communications, and avoid using children as messengers.*

Balancing Need for Communication and Boundaries

Profiles of interparent communication will vary from family to family. *The frequency, depth, and methods of communication should be determined by the degree of conflict between parents.* For example, cooperative parents can have more open communications with a less restrictive boundary. At the other end of the spectrum, parents with histories of domestic violence may have protection orders that limit or restrict interparent communication. Either way, children will benefit when parents have appropriate information for them to coordinate time schedules, support school and extracurricular activities, and have critical information for decision-making and problem-solving.

— Worksheet —

Co-parenting Communication

Parents Should Get Some Information on Their Own

Parents should not rely on each other for information that is independently available to them. For example, each parent can get game schedules from coaches and school information directly from schools. Schools typically have online access to school progress and homework assignments for younger students.

Notes: _____

Select Methods for Communicating

Communication options include texting, email messages, telephone conversations, face-to-face discussions, or meeting with a neutral third party. There are also a variety of smartphone apps. Search your app store by entering "co-parenting." Some parents may prefer texting as the primary medium for its convenience and because it maintains a record of the communications.

Notes: _____

Make a List of Parenting Topics

Important parenting discussion topics should reflect shared parental values. Discussion topics might include: healthcare, school, extracurricular activities, upcoming events, requests for schedule adjustments, notifications of being late for an exchange, decision-making, and problem-solving.

Notes: _____

Matching Methods with Purposes of Communication

Effective co-parenting communication can be enhanced by matching the methods with the purposes of communication. Being late for exchanges of the children or health care emergencies requires immediate communication such as a phone call or a text message. On the other hand, routine information sharing could be done via emails or sharing documents by mail or in person. Examples include sharing schedules of extracurricular activities or school events. In depth decision-making or problem-solving discussions might best be accomplished by talking in person or meeting with a mediator or therapist.

Notes: _____

— Worksheet —

Tips for High-Conflict Parents

Stop Text-Messaging Wars

All too often, text messages between high-conflict parents become an extension of litigation, as text messages are presented as evidence supporting allegations against one another. Long scrolling texts are read over and over again serving only to inflame the spirit. Offensive text messages are shared with conflict-support groups, counterarguments are made, and gotcha events are declared. *Genuinely attending to the needs of children gets lost in these text-messaging wars.*

Notes: _____

Stop Chasing Fault-Based Solutions

Conflicted parents will have two competing needs: The first is to prove fault in the other parent and then seek resolution based on those proven faults. The other is to seek co-parenting solutions for the children. Parents can get stuck in patterns of blame and fault-finding that will paralyze effective parenting. Pursuing fault-based solutions tends to trigger defensiveness and counter claims of fault.

Notes: _____

Disengage When Overwhelmed

Parents should catch themselves and disengage from communicating when they are at the point of being too stressed to be productive.

Notes: _____

Stay Focused on the Children

Parents should review the section on "Disengaging from Parent Conflict" describing how interparent conflict interferes with effective parenting. Parents should also review the Little Chair Exercise. It will help to see the needs of the children more clearly.

Notes: _____

Try Crafting Fault-Free Solutions

Start by declaring a value-based aspiration for the children, such as the children doing well in school. No longer asserting fault about the past, attention is redirected to finding fault-free solutions in the future, such as both parents helping with homework.

Notes: _____

Use Co-parenting Phone App

There are a variety of useful co-parenting phone apps. Parents can access their time-sharing schedule, names of doctors, clothing sizes, and dates for activities, events, and appointments for the children. Check your phone's app store.

Notes: _____

Seek Third-Party Assistance

There are professionals who can help: counselors, mediators, co-parenting coordinators, family therapists. Parents can agree to get help privately or petition the Court for a Court order to do so.

Notes: _____

Cautiously Introducing New Partners

GOAL: For parents to know the risks of introducing new partners too soon or too frequently and to introduce new partners with caution

Studies tell us that most parents will eventually take on new partners. Some will just date. Some will cohabitate. Some will remarry and some will do it multiple times. Studies also tell us that *some children find their parents' re-partnering to be more painful than their breakup.* At the same time, it is also important to be aware that many children do, in fact, ultimately enjoy the attentive care of two sets of parents. These children are free to love and be loved by four caring adults who provide an abundance of nurturing and support. This potential does indeed exist. Surely, an ideal worth pursuing!

— *Checklist* —

Reasons to Cautiously Introduce New Partners

Grief Interferes with Acceptance of New Partner

Grief is a natural response to parental breakups. Child reactions will differ by age. Toddlers and preschool age children may become anxious, cling, or act out. Older children may become angry, oppositional, withdrawn, take sides, or struggle with loyalty conflicts. It takes time to absorb and deal with the breakup and the life changes that come with it. *Adjusting to a new partner will be difficult while in a state of grief.*

Reunification Fantasy

Many children, especially young children, will have a private fantasy that their parents will reunite one day. They might hold on to this for years to come. *How do they welcome a new partner when they are still hoping for a reunification?*

71

Allow Time to Heal

Most experts advise that it takes a year or two before children are ready to absorb a new partner into their lives. Why? Children are often overloaded with adjustment challenges. There is a slow process of coming to accept the reality of the breakup followed by a list of abrupt life changes, such as living in two homes, relocating, changing schools, and moving away from extended family and friends. It just takes time.

Avoid Threats to Parental Status

Parents are likely to feel emotionally overwhelmed when the other parent introduces a new partner to the children. This is especially true for those breakups perceived to have been caused by an affair. Not only will these people be seen as having broken up a family, they will then be viewed as a threat to their parental status as mom or dad. Such grieving parents may not be able to hide or control their resentment. Quickly moving children into new stepfamilies with new partners will intensify conflict between parents and push the children into loyalty conflicts.

Stream of New Partners

Research indicated that *children are adversely affected by having a stream of new partners* enter and subsequently leave their lives. Sometimes they become attached to new partners and grieve the loss when they leave. The flow of new partners entering the lives of children often serves as perpetual reminders that mom or dad is showing way more interest in their new partners than they are in them. *This leaves them feeling abandoned and unwanted.* They are likely to become resentful of new partners.

Appreciate Differences in Readiness

Parents will be far more ready than children to take on a new partner. One or both parents may have emotionally withdrawn for years. They may have been planning the breakup for a long time. Some will have been dating and planning to re-partner as soon as the divorce is final. *Such parents will be excited, and in a hurry to move on. All the while the children are still grieving and hoping their parents stay together.* The difference: Parents are ready. Children are not!

Avoid Asking Children to Approve Dating Plans

Perhaps with good intentions, many parents will ask for a child's approval to have a new partner move in or to join them during their time together. *Parents should appreciate getting a child to approve of dating plans may be seen by the child as an act of betrayal to the other parent.* This puts children right in the middle of parental conflict, as they will be named as the source of giving the okay. They are likely to feel guilt, worry, fear, and stress from being put in the middle.

— Checklist —

Parental Dating Commitments

❏ Accept that one or both parents are likely to find a new partner

❏ Give children a year or two before introducing a new partner

❏ Avoid introducing children to casual dates

❏ Introduce new partners by name, not as mom or dad

❏ Let the other parent know that you are dating. Give a name

❏ Take small steps: introduction, lunch, visit a park, dinner, etc.

❏ Don't ask the children to keep secrets about dating

❏ Don't quiz the children about the other parent's new partner

❏ Primary parenting is provided by the natural parents

Helping Children Express Feelings with Words

GOAL: For parents to help their children be aware of and express their feelings in healthy ways

Using Words Instead of Behavior

Learning to talk about feelings is an important life skill for young children. When faced with disturbing life circumstances, such as a parental breakup or school problems, young children are likely to become overwhelmed with disturbing feelings. *Unable to understand or control their feelings, they may be inclined to act them out.* Temper tantrums and acting out behaviors are, in turn, likely to attract negative responses, both at home and at school. This will only add to their distress. Talking about feelings can be turned into a family routine. A feeling chart can be passed around with everyone taking a turn describing a good and a bad feeling they had during their day.

Step 1: Name That Feeling

Help children learn a vocabulary of feeling words as a first step in identifying their own feelings. *Children as young as three years old will be ready to learn how to talk about their feelings.* Have them view and name the feelings presented on the Feeling Chart in this section.

After learning the names of feelings, they will be ready to identify feelings they might be experiencing in any given moment. They could identify a feeling by simply naming the feeling or pointing to the feeling on the chart. Let them know they might be experiencing more than one feeling at a time.

Notes: _____

Step 2: How Big Is That Feeling?

Help children learn the skill of describing the intensity of their feelings. Explain to them that feelings come in different sizes. Try using a balloon inflated to different sizes to demonstrate this point. Parents or children could inflate the balloon to describe the size or intensity of their feelings. Children should indicate when the balloon size matches the size of their feeling. An alternative is to have children draw a single feeling face with three different sizes (small, medium, large) on a whiteboard or paper. Help children identify the physical, mental, and behavioral characteristics of a feeling: Physical sensations—*"I have butterflies in my belly."* Mental thoughts—*"I keep worrying about a test."* Behavior—*"I can't sit still."*

Notes: _____

Step 3: What Made You Feel That Way?

Have children identify the circumstances that triggered feelings within them. Help them see the difference between a feeling and a reaction. For example, children may have hurt feelings that may lead them to hit a sibling.

Notes: _____

Step 4: Vent Bad Feelings by Talking

Teach children the skill of talking about feelings. Be patient and get them to do most of the talking. The goal is to have them experience an emotional catharsis, a venting of feelings. Once feelings are vented, children will be less likely to act out their feelings. Learning skills to express and expel bad feelings without acting out will help children explore new ways to solve their problems.

Notes: _____

Feeling Chart: Name That Feeling

Happy

Sad

Mad

Worried

Nervous

Scared

Proud

Surprised

Disappointed

Hurt

Shy

Confused

Conflict-Free Exchanges of the Children

GOAL: For parents to exchange the children without exposing them to interparent conflict

A parental breakup will forever change the structure of a family in ways that force significant adjustment challenges upon the children. Once parents have separated, children must accommodate to living in two separate homes. *Exchanges will become a permanent feature of family living,* as children journey back and forth between their two households. Most children will be exchanged once or twice a week while others may be exchanged every day. Two big events will occur at each exchange: Children will be exchanged, and parents will encounter each other. Exchanges may be the only time that parents are in each other's presence. It is critical to the well-being of children for parents to establish effective, efficient, and child-centered exchanges. *Parents should commit to having exchanges serve one singular purpose: To exchange the children. And nothing more!*

— Worksheet —
Conflict-Free Exchanges

Recognize the Risk

For parents who are upset with each other, exchanges can be a flashpoint for interparent conflict. And, of course, children will be right in the middle of it. If an exchange goes badly, the children are also likely to be left to spend the next few days with hurt, angry, or anxious parents.

Note: _____

Don't Do It!

During the process of being exchanged from one parent to the other, children are most at risk for being exposed to parental conflict. Parents may have a powerful temptation to use the exchanges to confront or vent adult grievances. This will make the exchange environment toxic for the children. This should be avoided at all costs. Don't do it!

Note: _____

Avoid Provocations with New Partner

Newly separated parents who bring or send their new partners to pick up the children will predictably upset the other parent. This will be especially true if the new partner is perceived to have caused the breakup. It may threaten the parental status of the vulnerable parent. Such provocations should be avoided.

Note: _____

Not a Time to Talk About the Taxes

Parents should commit to keeping exchanges exclusively about exchanging the children. This is not the time to discuss tax deductions, child support, express grievances, or confront them about a new partner. All worthy topics, perhaps—just not in front of the children. Find or create other opportunities to do so.

Note: _____

Be Organized and On Time

Parents should try to turn exchanges into predictable routines. Children should be packed and ready to go for the exchange time. Be on time. Not showing or being chronically late or unprepared will bring unnecessary stress into the exchange. Regularly scheduled exchange times will help everyone adjust to this critical routine. Give the courtesy of providing advanced notice if changes are made to pick up or drop off times.

Note: _____

Let the Children Witness Civility

Children will feel parental tension at exchanges, even if no words are spoken. Do this for the children: Say hello to each other. The sending parent offers a brief positive report on the children, such as *"Billy scored a goal in his soccer game."* The receiving parent acknowledges Billy's success and both parents say *"Goodbye."* This could be done in as little as sixty seconds. Let the children witness civility and mutual respect.

Note: _____

Give Children a Little Time to Adjust to Transitions

Parents are likely to notice that their children may be upset or withdrawn when they receive them from the other parent. With each exchange, children must go through the adjustment of emotionally detaching from one parent and re-attaching to the next parent. The emotional culture of each home can be very different or intensely conflicted. They need a little time and space to adjust. Help them find soothing adjustment activities.

Note: _____

Manage Interparent Contact Time and Boundaries

Exchanges bring parents together. How much time and space they share together at an exchange with the children should be determined by the intensity of their conflict. For example, cooperative parents might enjoy lunch together with the children while high-conflict parents might have brief curbside exchanges. It can evolve over time.

Note: _____

Detail Exchanges in Court Orders

High-conflict parents should make detailed exchange plans in their official parenting plans filed in Family Court. Such Court orders can detail scheduled times, locations, driving responsibilities, change notifications, cancellations, or other important details.

Note: _____

Reduce Number of Exchanges

Frequent exchanges between high-conflict parents increases the risk to children. Such parents should seek to minimize the number of exchanges.

Note: _____

Use Neutral Exchanges

High-conflict parents should consider exchanges at neutral locations, such as at school or daycare. One parent takes the child to school and the other parent picks up the child after school. Such exchanges occur without parent contact.

Note: _____

Improving Coping Skills of Children

GOAL: For parents to develop resiliency in their children by enhancing their coping skills

Parental breakups will bring many adjustment challenges to children. Family life, as they had known it, will be forever changed. They may lose contact with grandparents, cousins, and other extended family members. Relocation will often separate children from friends in the community and at school. Grief reactions will be common. Parents should be aware that grief does not always appear as sadness. Sometimes grief will manifest in oppositional behavior, social withdrawal, and even anger—especially among adolescents. Children will be challenged by many new beginnings: potentially moving into a new home, a new neighborhood, and a new school. They must adjust to new social groups at school and in the neighborhood. Some children will be overloaded with more changes than they can endure. *Parents can help their children to adjust to their family changes and find stress relief by expanding and improving their coping skills.*

— Worksheet —
Helpful Coping Skills for Children

Processing Grief

Children can be *expected to have intermittent episodes of grief* that will come and go in waves of intense feelings. *Avoid dismissing those feelings. Instead encourage children to describe them,* allowing for an emotional venting or catharsis. Acknowledge and validate their feelings, as it is a necessary step towards acceptance. Then redirect their focus back into the moment—something fun or engaging.

Note: _____

Expressing Themselves Respectfully

Stressed children might either hide their feelings or act them out—sometimes in disrespectful ways. Parents should encourage children to express themselves, but to do it in a respectful manner. Introduce them to this catchy slogan: *"Say what you mean, but don't say it in a mean way."* Young children should be encouraged to use "nice" words and a "nice" tone. Older children should be invited to offer their views on important decisions but should be reminded that their parents will have the final say.

Note: _____

Improving Self-Control

Children stressed by parental breakups are likely to exhibit various forms of acting out behavior. When the intensity of acting out reaches its peak, they will not have access to the parts of the brain that provide executive functions needed for self-control. It would be best at those times to have children take a "calm down" timeout, staying as long as it takes to calm down. Once they are calm, they often express remorse. These will be the teachable moments, a time to review how they might have responded more appropriately. *Explore how the acting out behavior might have been an expression of grief.*

Note: _____

Respectful Refusal Skills

Children with highly conflicted parents will benefit from learning respectful refusal skills. For example, children asked to call the other parent to notify them that they will be returned late could simply state: "Mom, or Dad, that makes me nervous. Could you please make the call instead?"

Note: _____

Knowing Their Own Thoughts and Feelings

Anxious children might be inclined to mirror the thoughts and feelings of others. Parents can demonstrate how everyone has their own thoughts and feelings with safe examples: Everyone has a favorite flavor of ice cream, a favorite TV show, subject in school, and so on. When it comes to larger issues, give children permission to think or feel differently than their parents. Let them know it's okay to do so.

Note: _____

Using an Authoritative Parenting Style

GOAL: For parents to apply effective techniques of authoritative parenting that emphasize clear expectations and sensitive parental supervision

Consider three parenting styles: A *permissive* parenting style avoids imposing rules and allows children to manage themselves. An *authoritarian* parenting style demands strict obedience with little room for discussion. An *authoritative* parenting style sets clear expectations, holds children to compliance with contingencies, helps develop insight and responsibility, and engages children in a supportive and nurturing manner. Research suggests that *an authoritative parenting style will likely result in children who are more independent, socially adjusted, academically successful, and well-behaved.* It was also found that children will benefit even if only one parent uses an authoritative parenting style. Permissive parenting was reported to have resulted in children having more internalizing problems and associated with risky behaviors. Authoritarian parenting has been reported to result in children with poor social skills, poor self-esteem, and higher levels of depression.

— Worksheet —

Characteristics of Authoritative Parenting

Provide Clear Expectations

Authoritative parenting begins with a clear list of expectations. This is an opportunity for both parents to draw from a list of shared values, such as: 1) Children are to be *respectful*—to parents and others, 2) *Do well in school*—maintain an average of 85 or better, 3) *Develop healthy habits*—Follow routines for morning wakeup, homework, and bedtime, and 4) *Be helpful*—Take out the trash on Tuesday.

Notes: _____

Establish Behavioral Contingencies

Parents are encouraged to make a list of privileges that children most enjoy. Then consider a system of earned privileges where their privileges are no longer automatic entitlements. Instead, privileges are to be earned daily, like getting paid at the end of a day's work. Loss of privileges, when they occur, would be for only one day. In a calm voice, let them know they are about to lose privileges. Avoid nagging or attempting to persuade children who become defiant. Simply suspend privileges for one day. Let them know they will have a chance to earn them back the very next day. *Emphasis should be made on children learning they have the power to get the outcome they desire by simply following the rules.*

Notes: _____

Facilitate Understanding and Responsibility

Start with a listening skills strategy called "Stop, Look, and Listen." Young children should be directed to stop what they are doing, stand in front of a parent making eye contact, and repeat what has been said to them. Parents would state the rules and ask children to repeat them. Parents should then ask children to describe the outcomes if they follow or fail to follow the rules. Help children take responsibility for outcomes resulting from their decisions. Parents can develop a menu of special rewards for sustained compliance, such as going to a movie for being fully compliant for one week. Parents should ask children who lost privileges to explain why they lost them and what they would need to do to get it right the next time. *Help them see how following the rules leads to trust and expanded privileges in the future.*

Notes: _____

Be Emotionally Supportive and Nurturing

This parenting style appreciates that painful emotions, such as grief or worry, may be behind bad behavior. Encourage children to share their feelings and thoughts. Without transferring authority to them, allow them to have input into the development of rules and contingencies. Research has suggested that parents *taking time to deeply admire children with validating statements of love and affection* had a very powerful effect on their sense of well-being and good behavior.

Notes: _____

Building Healthy Support Systems

GOAL: For parents to establish healthy support systems for themselves and their children

The research on children of divorce has documented that family breakups introduce stress and challenges for both parents and children. The research has also found that the quality and speed of adjustment varied greatly from family to family based, in part, on the degree to which they took advantage of the supportive resources that were available to them. Parents are encouraged to work on building healthy support systems. Doing so will enhance their ability to navigate their way to a healthy outcome for themselves and their children. *This section will help parents locate supportive resources in their families, among their friends, in their communities, and online.*

— Worksheet —

Building Healthy Support Systems

Teach Others How to Be Supportive

Family and friends really want to help. However, *sometimes they need guidance on where to draw the boundary lines.* Often parents just need someone to listen to them and not take over their problems. With good intention, parents may get too much advice from too many people. That can be overwhelming. There will be times when parents just need to have a little quiet time where they are not talking about their problems. Teaching others how to be helpful will enrich the quality of support received from others.

Notes: _____

Avoid Tribal Warfare

Parents would be well advised to avoid formulating or feeding into the development of support systems that advance interfamily tribal warfare. Such support systems are saturated with drama that promotes conflict rather than relieving it. It can feed into chronic litigation. Such support teams are likely to inflame and ultimately exhaust parents emotionally and financially. Posting allegations and disputes publicly on social media will likely expand the network of warriors on both sides. It will be hard to put these fires out. *Having others take sides can make parents feel good but may not be helpful in the long run.*

Notes: _____

Individual or Family Therapy

Both parents and children can benefit from individual counseling or psychotherapy. Children often enjoy a safe place to talk about their feelings. Family therapy is an alternative that focuses on adjusting family relationships to bring relief to children. For example, *improving the co-parenting relationship can bring relief to children.* Seeing each parent alone with the children can bring relief as well. Sometimes including extended family members, such as grandparents providing childcare while parents are at work, can be helpful. Family therapy would be helpful for adjustments needed in the formulation of stepfamilies.

Notes: _____

Community-Based Support Groups

An internet search of community resources can help parents find support groups such as Alcoholics Anonymous; Narcotics Anonymous; Al-Anon; parenting children with special needs; and programs for children, such as arts, scouts, achievement, dance, athletics, and many more.

Notes: _____

School-Based Support

Parents may want to let teachers know that the children might be going through a stressful time. This will help teachers support the children at school. Parents may find that schools provide supportive counseling to children. Some schools will have special programs for children who are going through a family breakup. Talking to the school principal or guidance counselor is a good place to start.

Notes: _____

— Resources —

Supportive Online Resources

Internet Search Topics

- ❏ AA or NA meetings near me
- ❏ Al-Anon meetings near me
- ❏ Alimony
- ❏ Adverse childhood experiences
- ❏ Anger management evaluations
- ❏ Anger management treatment
- ❏ Authoritative parenting
- ❏ Autism and divorced parents
- ❏ ADHD and divorced parents
- ❏ Child abuse hotline
- ❏ Child custody plans by age
- ❏ Child custody evaluations
- ❏ Child custody mediation
- ❏ Child executive functioning skills
- ❏ Child protective services
- ❏ Child support
- ❏ Children of divorce
- ❏ Collaborative law
- ❏ Cooperative parenting
- ❏ Co-parenting counseling or coordination
- ❏ Dialectical behavior therapy
- ❏ Domestic violence hotline and shelters
- ❏ Drug and alcohol evaluations
- ❏ Drug and alcohol treatment
- ❏ Domestic violence
- ❏ Effects of divorce on children
- ❏ Emotional intelligence

- ❏ Family law attorney near me
- ❏ Family therapy
- ❏ Fathers' rights
- ❏ Grandparents rights
- ❏ Guardian ad litem
- ❏ Healthy habits for children
- ❏ Introducing new partners to children
- ❏ Joint or shared physical custody
- ❏ Legal vs. physical custody
- ❏ Long-distance parenting
- ❏ Marital affairs and divorce
- ❏ Mindfulness
- ❏ Parallel parenting
- ❏ Parent alienation
- ❏ Parent-child enmeshment
- ❏ Parent-child reunification therapy
- ❏ Parent divorce education
- ❏ Parents in prison
- ❏ Resilient children
- ❏ Restraining court orders
- ❏ Same-sex divorce
- ❏ Sample child custody orders
- ❏ Sleep training for children
- ❏ Stepfamilies, stepsiblings, half siblings
- ❏ Supervised visitation
- ❏ Teen pregnancies
- ❏ Therapists near me
- ❏ Trauma therapy for adults and children

YouTube Searches

- Bedtime stories for children
- Children expressing anger
- Children talking about feelings
- Mindfulness in children
- Muppets on divorce, grief
- Muppets on addiction, parent incarceration
- Muppets on just about anything
- Nurturing children
- Talking to children about divorce
- Telling children we are getting divorced
- Unusually satisfying videos
- Yoga for children

Smartphone App Store

- ADHD
- Alimony calculator
- Child support calculator
- Cognitive behavior therapy for depression
- Co-parenting apps: AppClose, WeParent
- Homework planner
- Nature sounds
- Mindfulness: Calm, Headspace
- Stress management
- Medical apps

Amazon Book Topics

- Books for children on divorce
- Books for parents on divorce
- Co-parenting after divorce
- Coping with divorce for women or men
- Children and executive function
- Children with special needs
- Divorce adjustment
- High-conflict parents
- Listening to children
- Parent alienation
- Parent-child reunification
- Safeguarding the well-being of children
- Self-confidence in children
- Self-control books for children

— Co-parent Worksheet —

Shared Family Transition Plan Part I: Shared View of Child Adjustment Problems

This form will help parents develop a shared view of possible adjustment problems experienced by their children. Parents should not dismiss the observations of the other parent, as children often cope by acting differently with each parent. Views from both parents will provide the most complete understanding of how children are coping.

Directions: List names of children in each age group. Parents should place a checkmark to indicate adjustment problems they have observed in their children. Add notes for clarification.

Infants & Toddlers (Birth to 2.5 Years of Age)

Names of children in this age group: _____

Mom Dad

❏ ❏ Sleep problems: _____

❏ ❏ Separation anxiety: _____

❏ ❏ Abandonment reactions: _____

❏ ❏ Other problems: _____

Insights by mom: _____

Insights by dad: _____

Preschool Children (3 to 5 Years of Age)

Names of children in this age group: _____

Mom Dad

❏ ❏ Self-blame: _____

❏ ❏ Acting-out: _____

❏ ❏ Other problems: _____

Insights by mom: _____

Insights by dad: _____

Early Elementary School Children (6 to 8 Years of Age)

Names of children in this age group: _____

Mom Dad

❏   ❏   School problems: _____

❏   ❏   Loyalty problems: _____

❏   ❏   Other problems: _____

Insights by mom: _____

Insights by dad: _____

Late Elementary School Children (9 to 12 Years of Age)

Names of children in this age group: _____

Mom Dad

❏   ❏   Identity problems: _____

❏   ❏   Taking sides: _____

❏   ❏   Other problems: _____

Insights by mom: _____

Insights by dad: _____

Adolescent Children (13 to 18 Years of Age)

Names of children in this age group: _____

Mom Dad

❏   ❏   Risky behavior: _____

❏   ❏   Relationship problems: _____

❏   ❏   Other problems: _____

Insights by mom: _____

Insights by dad: _____

Assessment of the Impact of Interparent Conflict

How might the above problems be an expression of parental conflict? _____

_____

_____

How might interparent conflict limit our ability to help our children? _____

_____

_____

— Co-parent Worksheet —

Shared Family Transition Plan Part II: Parents Working Together to Help Their Children

After completing their individual family transition plans, parents should work together to develop a shared plan designed to ensure the healthy adjustment of their children as they experience the breakup of their parents. The fifteen positive steps have been organized into three ways children will likely benefit from the support of their parents. Each parent should review the goals and place a checkmark to indicate their commitment to implementing each of the helpful strategies. They should use the "Weekly Self-Monitoring Guide" to stay focused on helping their children.

Goals & Helpful Strategies

Mom	Dad	GOAL: Reduce Initial and Transitional Family Stress
❏	❏	Telling the Children
❏	❏	Helping Children Express Their Feelings with Words
❏	❏	Seeing Problems Through the Eyes of a Child
❏	❏	Conflict-Free Exchanges of the Children
❏	❏	Keeping Children Out of the Middle

Mom	Dad	GOAL: Improve Long-Term Family Stability
❏	❏	Vision of a Healthy Two-Home Family
❏	❏	Parents Taking Care of Themselves
❏	❏	Disengaging from Parent Conflict
❏	❏	Resetting Parenting Boundaries
❏	❏	Co-parenting Communication
❏	❏	Cautiously Introducing New Partners

Mom	Dad	GOAL: Increase Stress Tolerance and Resiliency
❏	❏	Improving Coping Skills of Children
❏	❏	Using an Authoritative Parenting Style
❏	❏	Building Healthy Support Systems

— *Single-Parent Worksheet* —

Weekly Self-Monitoring Guide

Having good intentions and a good plan will not be enough to guarantee that the desired outcome will be achieved. This weekly self-monitoring form will help parents keep their actions in alignment with their plans. Answer yes or no to each question. For no answers, write self-improvement statements at the bottom of the page. Keep a journal of your weekly assessments and self-improvement commitments.

Weekly Self-Monitoring Questions

Yes	No	
❏	❏	Am I guided by and working toward a vision of a healthy two-home family?
❏	❏	Am I adequately taking care of myself?
❏	❏	Am I using strategies to disengage from conflict and engage in cooperative co-parenting?
❏	❏	Am I using the Little Chair Exercise to see my children's perspective?
❏	❏	Am I doing my part to keep children out of the middle of parental conflict?
❏	❏	Am I aware of Court-connected interventions to manage safety issues?
❏	❏	Am I talking to my children about family changes in a child-sensitive manner?
❏	❏	Am I maintaining healthy boundaries for myself and honoring boundaries of the other parent?
❏	❏	Am I doing my part to keep conflict out of our co-parenting communications?
❏	❏	Am I following guidance on cautiously introducing new partners to my children?
❏	❏	Am I encouraging and helping my children to verbally express their thoughts and feelings?
❏	❏	Am I doing my part in keeping exchanges free of parent conflict?
❏	❏	Am I helping my children to improve their coping skills?
❏	❏	Am I using strategies of the authoritative parenting style?
❏	❏	Am I maintaining healthy support systems for myself and my children?
❏	❏	I take responsibility for doing my part: How can I improve my efforts? _____

"Children seldom misquote. In fact,
they usually repeat word for word
what you shouldn't have said."
— Unknown Author

Made in the USA
Monee, IL
23 December 2024

75305830R00059